FARMING

FOR

FUEL

FARMING
FOR
FUEL

The Political Economy of Energy Sources in the United States

Folke Dovring

PRAEGER

New York
Westport, Connecticut
London

Library of Congress Cataloging-in-Publication Data

Dovring, Folke.
    Farming for fuel : the political economy of energy sources in the
  United States / Folke Dovring.
        p.   cm.
      Bibliography: p.
      Includes index.
      ISBN 0-275-93008-4 (alk. paper)
        1. Biomass energy industries—Government policy—United States.
2. Energy crops industry—Government policy—United States.
3. Agriculture and energy—Government policy—United States.
4. Agriculture and state—United States.   5. Energy policy—United
States.   I. Title.
HD9502.5.B543U625   1988
333.76—dc19
87-38479

Library of Congress Catalog Card Number: 87-38479

ISBN: 0-275-93008-4

First published in 1988

Praeger Publishers, One Madison Avenue, New York, NY 10010
A division of Greenwood Press, Inc.

Printed in the United States of America

The paper used in this book complies with the
Permanent Paper Standard issued by the National
Information Standards Organization (Z39.48-1984).

10 9 8 7 6 5 4 3 2 1

CONTENTS

Tables and Figures   vii

Preface   ix

1   Four Problems—One Solution   1

2   The Petroleum Age   5

3   Replacing Petroleum: The Many Choices   17

4   Gasohol—A Blind Alley   33

5   Biomass Production as Land-Use
         Diversification   47

6   Biomass Production as Soil Conservation   67

7   Methanol Raw Materials: Possible Supplies
         and Costs   81

8   Converting Biomass to Methanol   97

9	Using Methanol in Vehicles	113
10	The Road Not Taken	123
References		133
Index		147
About the Author		151

TABLES AND FIGURES

TABLES

2.1   Energy Use in the U.S. Economy, Selected
       Years 1850–1985. Total Btu, Distribution
       among Main Energy Sources, and Ratio of
       Consumption over Production   8

5.1   Major Uses of Cropland, United States   50

5.2   Base Acreage Diverted from Production under
       Federal Farm Programs, United States   62

10.1   Consumption per Capita of Total Energy and
       of Motor Gasoline, Selected Countries and
       Years   131

FIGURES

5.1   U.S. Land Base in 1977   49

6.1   Average Annual Cropland Erosion, 1982   70

6.2   Major Areas of Groundwater Mining   73

PREFACE

A statesman ahead of his time said in the late 1970s that he thought of those years as "a hinge of history." Something is turning; we shall have to chart and accept new directions. An obvious case is the energy system. Petroleum and natural gas will become more and more expensive until they run out of our reach. There are many options for replacing these fund resources, which were very convenient when they were cheap.

In the large fabric of society, the energy system interacts with many other things, and these in turn are interdependent. A solution to the energy problem can therefore not be found in isolation. The proposal made in this book is that the best future mainstay of energy supply in the United States is methanol, eventually to be produced entirely from biomass. This will solve not only the problems of energy supply and vulnerable oil imports but also the farm problems of surplus production, low prices, and soil erosion and the ecological ones of air pollution and eventual overheating of the atmosphere.

The consequences of this solution are revolutionary, yet the changes can be phased in gradually. Only by accepting changes of such sweeping nature can we solve multiple interacting problems in a way that leads to a stable future.

FARMING
FOR
FUEL

1

FOUR PROBLEMS—ONE SOLUTION

Petroleum imports.
Farm surplus production.
Soil conservation.
Air pollution.
What have these four problems in common? They all can be solved or
greatly reduced by one single large policy departure: large-scale production of methanol (wood alcohol) from biomass, to become a mainstay
of the energy system of the United States. As the road fuel of choice,
methanol from biomass could replace petroleum imports, remove surplus farm production, reduce air pollution, and improve the conservation of farmlands from erosion. Methanol has long been recognized as
a safe and efficient fuel in racing cars, as on the Indianapolis 500 speed-
way.

Petroleum imports have been with us since the 1950s and on two
occasions, 1973–1974 and 1979–1981, became a burden and a danger
because of price action by a cartel ruled from foreign countries. In both
of these periods the price shocks from the oil market let loose "stagflation," an unprecedented combination of recession and inflation. The last
several years may have given the public the impression that the oil problem has gone away because the countries forming the OPEC (Organization of Petroleum Exporting Countries) cartel could not maintain
disciplined joint action. This would be an illusion. The oil problem was
merely dormant and just began to be felt again in 1987. The prospect
is for prices to rise continuously because many of the petroleum exporting countries have limited reserves. As their own industry grows
and their reserves become smaller, one after another of these countries

will phase out oil exports, keeping remaining reserves for their own needs. Toward the year 2000 only countries around the Persian Gulf will export petroleum. The basis for cartel action will then be stronger than ever and the danger greater that the United States may be manipulated both economically and politically by small, unstable, and distant states, having little in common with us except for petroleum. Price action apart, the military and political costs of protecting the oil supplies would then be a growing burden on our economy. As yet, such costs are not factored into the cost of petroleum: therefore, gasoline seems cheaper than it is.

The oil problem is shouting for a solution. With problems of such character and magnitude, the solutions must be planned long in advance. The policy of the early 1980s has lost us precious time. Whatever has to be done must now be done at shorter notice and with less room for maneuvering.

Farm surplus production has been with us for a long time. The resource base for agricultural production in the United States is unusually large and has always had the potential for producing more than existing markets are able and willing to take. There were some policy beginnings in the 1920s, when U.S. agriculture was depressed even before the whole country was, and again in the New Deal legislation of the 1930s. Wartime shortages, prolonged through the Korean conflict of the early 1950s, delayed the agricultural overproduction problem, but it came out in the open in earnest in the middle of the 1950s.

Since then there has been a succession of federal programs to help farmers. None of these programs has been entirely successful, and they all have cost the federal treasury and the taxpayers huge sums of money. It is likely that consumers got a hidden benefit from accelerating productivity development in agriculture. Lessened uncertainty led to more willingness on the part of farmers to invest in the means of raising productivity. These gains may well have outweighed the treasury costs of supports, but they have not been understood in this light. Not much of this effect, however, is likely in the future. In recent years, federal farm supports have cost about $20–$25 billion a year. The most recent version of the farm bill threatens to become even more expensive in fiscal terms despite all proclaimed intentions of reducing the federal budget deficit and approaching a balanced federal budget. Even so, farmers are not very well served by these programs. They depend on legislation from year to year and are constantly laboring under the threat that the surplus may come back next year and depress their prices, leading to more and more farm bankruptcies.

A long-term, reliable solution to the farm surplus production problem should include an element of land-use diversification. Instead of withholding some acreage from crop production on an ad hoc, year-to-year basis, large acreages should be permanently removed from use in the production of food and fiber crops. So far, all proposals for new land uses in agriculture have been for specialty crops such as those supplying high-quality lubricants for automobile engines or certain plants used in the pharmaceutical and cosmetics industries. All such additional crops occupy only small acreages and do little to remedy the rising surplus capacity of agriculture. Luxury items such as Christmas trees and fancy vegetables have not been very helpful either for the reduction of land in basic agricultural production.

The agricultural experiment stations, in their attempts to help farmers, usually think of nothing better than to increase agricultural productivity, as a means of lowering unit costs of production, to make U.S. farmers' products more price competitive on foreign markets. Minor as this avenue of improvement may be in the near term, it will do little to help the individual farmer. Increasing productivity usually means also increasing output. The lower costs will then be met by lower international prices. The need for federal farm support would continue, including the large-scale idling of farmland. The set-aside land is merely prohibited from producing; it is not diverted into other production.

The only land-use diversification that would really remove large parts of surplus capacity for food and fiber production would be diversification for the production of fuel feedstocks. Merely planting trees for timber will not answer, for the timber markets are on the whole adequately supplied. Timber lands also represent lower land values than croplands and pasture lands; and the transition to much more woodland would entail huge capital losses, to be made up by the federal treasury or to be absorbed by individuals going bankrupt.

As the following chapters will show, production of biomass (wood and hay) for energy production could absorb very large acreages that would still be producing considerable values to landowners. Agricultural production for food and fiber could then be restricted to more productive lands. This would also remove from cropping and pasture large acreages that are sloping or otherwise vulnerable to erosion. Permanent vegetation of trees or grasses or both would mean that vulnerable sites would be tilled only at long intervals, if at all. This would greatly reduce soil erosion, a problem because it removes some of the productive power of our farmlands and because it overloads running water with silt, causing reservoirs and dam sites to fill up more rapidly. When that happens, we must either dredge such sites or replace them with new ones. Either case increases the cost of the purpose for which the reservoirs and dams have been built. Increased silt load in the rivers also complicates flood control.

The fourth problem mentioned above is air pollution in the cities. Much of it is caused by exhausts from automobile engines. In Los Angeles, the reduction of carbon emissions (soot) by burning gasoline and diesel fuel at higher temperatures increased the formation of nitrates. The giant city thus exchanged one kind of smog for another one. The radical approach to air pollution would be to use fuels that do not pollute or that pollute much less. Methanol has the advantage of polluting much less because it burns more completely. The inherent heat value of a volume unit of methanol is half that of the same volume unit of gasoline, but the propulsion value is 60 percent of that of gasoline because methanol burns more completely, thus leaving behind less of anything that might foul the air people have to breathe.

To solve or mitigate four major problems by a single large policy departure is indeed unusual and would certainly go a long way to recommend such a proposal. We may however add one more problem that the biomass energy path will help solve: the distant—but no longer very distant—threat of overloading the atmosphere with so much carbon and so much waste heat that we get a greenhouse effect. Overwarming the atmosphere would change the climates and melt the ice caps on Greenland and Antarctica. Coastal plains and cities would then be lost to rising ocean levels. It does not help to say that the reserves of fossil coal are still very large, for we could never burn all that without letting loose the greenhouse effect. Some rumors talk about gigantic untapped masses of natural gas at great depth in the bowels of the earth. Even if this were to prove true, we should make up our minds never to tap these reserves lest we ruin our planet.

Biomass energy, by contrast, will not add any new carbon to the atmosphere, and its waste heat will be no more than the solar heat previously absorbed to build up the biomass. Such energy sources will merely recycle the same carbon over and over again with the help of fresh sunshine as the only energy source; the same goes for solar heat being used in this way. This is true both for natural biomass and for hydrocarbons produced by aid of artificial chlorophyll. Removing the threat of overheating from the atmosphere is all the more important because it is not the only threat to the soundness of the entire ecosphere. Other threats will have to be dealt with on their terms, and even biomass energy is not entirely without ecological hazards even though they are much smaller than those from fossil coal and primal gas.

Having justified the use of biomass energy in general and methanol specifically, it remains to emphasize that time is of the essence. Huge new capital investments cannot be generated quickly. If we wait until the price proportions are favorable, these investments will not be assembled in time. The problem should have been taken in hand for long-term planning before now. Every year that elapses without concerted policy action will only make the problem more difficult later on.

2

THE PETROLEUM AGE

The time span in modern history when fossil liquid and gaseous hydro-carbons are the mainstay of energy supply is short by any standards of comparative history. Wood, wind, and coal have each covered longer periods in the role of leading energy source. But for most modern people it is well-nigh impossible to visualize what it will mean when oil fades from the picture, as it will within decades. Most people alive today were born during the petroleum age, and they can not imagine themselves outliving it.

The first that we must do when debating the future of energy supply is to take in the trivial truth that fossil oil—petroleum—will become a minor energy source within a short time. What we can do to obtain motor fuel will then depend on what the alternative fuels are or are perceived to be. The costs of more expensive fuels must be weighed against the costs of living with less motor fuel. Only in part will this be decided by pure cost arguments. The cost arguments will often be de-flected by vested interests and wishful thinking.

That the supply of oil will be exhausted can be shown rather easily. Just when this will happen is open to a little more disagreement. The issue begins to be complicated when we discuss alternatives.

BEFORE PETROLEUM

For use on land, wood fuel was long the main source of fire and other immediate energy. In this forest rich country, fuel wood was nearly the only heat source in the 1600s and 1700s. It outweighed all the fossil sources until the 1880s.

Coal extraction in the United States began about 1800. It increased through the 1800s and reached a plateau about 1916. It remained on that plateau magnitude, with variations, until recently. The drive to save on oil since 1973 led to some increase in coal mining. In this country coal was a larger power source than oil and natural gas until 1948. In other countries, the chronological sequences have been different. Coal became prominent in England much earlier than anywhere else.

These comparisons, drawn for the United States from *The Historical Statistics of the United States*, refer to the heat values of the fuels as they were produced. Outside all such calculations lies the use of wind power. It has had some application, more than negligible at the time, for minor industrial tasks such as flour milling and for pumping water from mines. Above all, wind was the main source of motive power for ships in the whole modern period, before the coming of steamships. Compared to the muscle powered rowing ships of Antiquity, the use of sails represented an enormous gain in economy. It rendered feasible international shipping from the age of discoveries to the later 1800s. Only about a hundred years ago did steam begin to propel more cargo than wind in transoceanic ships. When grain began to move in large quantities into Europe from the United States and Australia, much of it was still carried by the great windjammers, ships capable of moving against the main direction of the wind by zig-zagging their course so as to capture variations in wind direction.

The age of wood still lingers in rural areas in large parts of low-income countries. In India, the problem of static supply and growing demand for rural household fuel has been dubbed "the other energy crisis."

A special case of an energy source becoming insufficient after its introduction as industrial fuel is peat. The Netherlands' start toward early industrialization in the 1600s was based on peat. That did not last because the power source was too limited (De Zeeuw 1978). Only much later could the Dutch resume industrialization based on imported fuel.

Coal was used a long time before it became a dominant energy source. Both for Britain and the United States, the age of coal must be reckoned from the time when it had become "the cutting edge" of industrial progress and land transportation. That places it from about 1700 in England and at least since the middle 1800s in the United States. For steel making, the age of coal in the United States began even earlier. Pennsylvania anthracite (now nearly all mined out) became a mainstay in the blast furnaces and caused the early concentration of steel making in the Pittsburgh area.

The date when petroleum began to be important cannot be established on purely quantitative grounds. Replacing coal in ships' motors and train engines was a convenience but hardly a breakthrough. Instead we should look to the role of petroleum as the source of motive power for road vehicles as the criterion of a "petroleum age." The horseless carriage may have been a butt of jokes originally. But when automobiles came on the assembly line, a true revolution was begun—in modes and costs of transportation, in location economics, and in lifestyles both practical and emotional. The age of petroleum can be said to date from about 1920, from the resumption of peacetime conditions after World War I. Selected data are shown in Table 2.1.

THE EARLY STAGES

Before 1859, petroleum had been scooped up by the bucketful from shallow wells into which it was seeping from surrounding earth or rock. Modern petroleum technology began with a bang just before the U.S. Civil War. An amateur engineer, drilling for oil as one might drill for water, hit a gusher in Pennsylvania—a very small gusher as later oil history goes, but still both a shocker and an eye opener. U.S. statistics show petroleum extraction with 2,000 barrels in 1859, 500,000 barrels in 1860, 5 1/4 million in 1870, 26 million in 1880, 64 million in 1900, and 443 million in 1920.

This explosive growth in output was small by current yardsticks. Annual use of crude oil in this country is now more than ten times the extraction of 1920. The early growth phases took place against the backdrop of estimates for proven reserves that continued to look very large. When such estimates began, in 1899, the proven reserve was nearly 50 times the extraction of that year. By 1920, the proportion had fallen to 16 times annual extraction but reserves continued to go up faster than extraction, in absolute quantity. This time and again gave the lie to early doomsayers who based their forecasts on past experience rather than on geological insights.

One immediate consequence of the unexpected windfall in cheap energy was an inability to know what to do with it all. Early uses included kerosene lamps and the greasing of factory machines. The latter was a great stride of progress because, unlike animal fats, petroleum lubricants do not become rancid. That had necessitated frequent relubrication in the age when animal fats were used as lubricants. The natural gasoline component of crude oil was at first a useless byproduct that was just allowed to flow away.

Thus the invention of the gasoline powered car motor came as a consequence of cheap fuel, not the other way around. This should give pause to reflect to those who maintain that market forces will call forth the needed energy resources. Cheap gasoline was not at first a response to market forces but a consequence of geological hazard, neither predicted nor predictable. Conversely, more market demand will not call forth any more oil than is actually present in the rocks.

Table 2.1
Energy Use in the U.S. Economy, Selected Years 1850–1985. Total Btu, Distribution among Main Energy Sources, and Ratio of Consumption over Production

Year	Total quads of Btu	Percent distribution by source:					Ratio of consump-tion
		Coal	Oil[a]	Gas	Other[b]	Wood	
1850	2.4	9	..	..	..	91	1.00
1870	4.0	27	0	..	..	73	.99
1890	7.0	59	2	3	0	36	.97
1910	16.6	77	6	3	3	11	.97
1930	23.7	57	26	8	3	6	.99
1950	35.2	35	39	19	4	3	1.01
1960	45.4	22	44	28	4	2	1.04
1970	67.6	19	44	32	4	1	1.08
1979[c]	78.9	19	47	26	8	..	1.24
1980	76.0	20	45	27	8	..	1.17
1982	70.8	22	43	26	9	..	1.11
1985	73.8	24	42	24	10	..	1.14

[a] Includes liquefied petroleum gas
[b] Mainly electricity from hydropower and nuclear power, recently also geothermal steam and sundry sources
[c] Peak year

Sources: 1850–1970 calculated from *Historical Statistics of the United States*, U.S. Government Publication, vol. 1, Table M76–92.
1979–85 from *Statistical Abstract of the United States*, U.S. Government Publication, 1987, Table 932, p. 542.

The cheap optimism of the early petroleum age is thus explicable if not for that sake justified. The facts were not as reassuring as they may have seemed, and a reassessment of the prospects was not far into the future.

GAUGING THE LIMITS

Simple reflection tells us that petroleum, like all extractible mineral resources, must be finite. There is some limit beyond which extraction must cease. The actual limits require insight into the geology of "rock oil," and such insight can be helped by observation of the rates at which new finds are made.

The basic work in regard to petroleum in the United States was made by M. King Hubbert and has been published by him since the 1950s. His observations relate to the continental United States, not including Alaska. Among his findings are that the rate of new oil discovery peaked in the 1930s and has been declining since then. Oil extraction, by contrast, continued to increase long after discovery had peaked. There must thus come a time when reserves will be drawn down so much that further increases in production will be unlikely. This maximum peak of extraction, Hubbert predicted, would occur between 1966 and 1971. It occurred in 1970. Thereafter, he argued, oil extraction would decline. In the downswing it would follow a curve that would resemble the mirror image of what had happened during the upswing. In the decades after 1970, extraction would first go down slowly, thereafter more rapidly, and, in a relatively long final stage, a much smaller volume of oil extraction would decline slower in absolute terms but still rapidly in relative terms.

The calculations show that of the entire extractible quantity, 80 percent would be extracted within 67 years (1932–1999), or in 61 years (1938–1999). All petroleum liquids are included in the latter case. The volume would fall rapidly during the 1990s. After the year 2000 annual extraction in the United States would be one-fourth or less of that in the peak of 1970. For the whole world, the peak would be in the 1990s, with 80 percent extracted in 56 years (1967–2023).

Hubbert's findings were at first met with incredulity, even among oil specialists. These people were so fascinated by the large volume of oil still known to be in the ground that they would not at first believe that an oil crisis could erupt in their lifetime. In their grandchildren's time, maybe, but that was too early to worry about, so the initial reaction went.

The petroleum people soon changed their outlook, because of the import statistics if for no other reasons. Since 1949 the United States has imported more petroleum than it has exported. In the 1970s, imports at times rose to about 40 percent of total consumption in the country. After a somewhat smaller role for oil imports in the early 1980s, imports are again on the rise and soon will reach the magnitude of the 1970s.

The general public has the greatest difficulty in visualizing the magnitudes and proportions involved. The 1920 level of extraction in the United States was ten times the level in 1890, a time when the car engine was still a technological fledgling. In recent years we have reached ten times the level of 1920 extraction—in annual consumption, not in extraction. The problem of advancing much beyond such a level is in part obscured by the varying estimates of oil reserves that the public is offered (Kerr 1981).

ESTIMATES AND PROJECTIONS

In gauging future supplies, Hubbert used a combination of geology, past experience of discovery, and prices in relation to national product. Many economists use only price and income data and so arrive at much more optimistic forecasts of what future oil supply may be (Netschert 1958; Pagoulatos et al., 1978). Ignoring geology makes such estimates worthless. About 1980 the notion that all we need for energy independence is free market prices had widespread publicity. This illusion was not directly supported by the petroleum experts, but most of the time they did not do enough to contradict such visions of the future; and unfounded oil optimism became official policy in the United States in the early 1980s.

The vision has faded. One reason was the experience with uncontrolled petroleum prices after decontrol was completed in early 1981, a half year earlier than anticipated (*The Petroleum Situation*, Chase Manhattan Bank, October 1977–April 1981). Other reasons to revise the outlook were in the generally deteriorating situation regarding oil supply. After the middle of the decade, energy policy again became an important part of the Washington agenda (Fri 1987).

The expectations that decontrol of oil prices would bring large new oil discoveries reflected some of the high estimates that had been advanced to refute Hubbert. These expectations for large new finds were not fulfilled. Bold geological hypotheses had been set forth about the consequences of an overthrust zone in the Rocky Mountain area and maybe a second one in the Appalachians. The former zone is, in fact, the explanation for the limited oil fields in Wyoming, but nothing of even that scope was discovered in the oil rush of the early 1980s. On the whole, drillings in the overthrust zone gave disappointing results.

Three things made oil extraction level off in the early 1980s instead of begin to decline: infield drillings, enhanced recovery of tertiary oil, and Alaska.

Infield drilling ("stripper" wells) means using the leftovers in the outskirts of old oil fields. High prices would render extraction profitable in many such sites that had not been attractive while prices were low, before 1973. The results of infield drilling are moderate; they do not represent any long-term answer to the fuel problem. When low prices returned to the oil markets in 1986 because of OPEC disarray, many of the small stripper wells had to be capped as unprofitable. Some of these may never open again because that could be done only when oil prices are so high that replacement energy sources are cheaper.

Enhanced recovery of tertiary oil means applying new technologies such as chemical solvents toward dislocating oil that is widely scattered in porous rocks (Garland 1979). Most of this tertiary oil is undoubtedly out of reach for economic exploiting. Reported claims of oil interests to have reached some breakthrough in enhanced-recovery techniques have been found premature in most cases.

Alaska was not included in Hubbert's calculations. Hopes rose high because of the single large find at Prudhoe Bay on the Alaska North Slope in 1970. The field came onstream in 1978, at very high cost because of both the trans-Alaska pipeline and the arctic climate. The field had an estimated extractible quantity of 10 billion barrels, which corresponds to two to three years of U.S. oil consumption. A substantial part of that has now been extracted. Subsequent exploration led to a second find near Prudhoe Bay, of only 100 million barrels (1 percent of the first find).

Offshore drilling around Alaska has been an economic disaster: from several dozen holes drilled, only one minor find was made. Several major attempts had to be abandoned after high costs had been incurred. The extreme case was at Mukluk, in the Beaufort Sea north of Alaska. One major partner in this venture, Sohio, had to write off $300 million as total loss. This raised Sohio's cost of exploration per barrel of newly found oil (in all locations) in that year to over $50 a barrel, clearly an unacceptable result. Other offshore exploration—around Florida, in the Atlantic east of New Jersey, around New England and farther northeast from there—has also led to very few positive results.

The causes of such disappointing results from renewed oil search are not hard to discover. U.S. petroleum experts know their job, and they had explored nearly all the really plausible sites early on, while oil was still cheap. Thus mainly the less plausible sites were left for the 1980s oil rush. Reported estimates of oil yet to be discovered in North America have also become smaller with time. The huge counter estimates offered as alternatives to Hubbert's are nowhere maintained. One of the most recent estimates is also among the least optimistic (Nehring and Van Driest 1981).

Even without such incidentals as the Mukluk failure, it is clear that the payoff to exploration is decreasing. Drilling in the continental United States is likely to cease being profitable about the year 2000 (Hall and Cleveland 1981). Other statistical analyses also show that discovery tends to proceed toward smaller and smaller finds (Menard and Sharman 1975). British material supports the same conclusion for discovery in the North Sea (J. L. Smith 1980).

But the petroleum experts do not give up easily. In face of all the signs that domestic oil sources will be dwindling, the oil experts still want to be "Making the best of oil search" (*Petroleum Economist*, July 1981, pp. 282–83) and to postpone as long as possible the eventual transition to other fuels. Again the reasons for this attitude are not hard to discern. The petroleum complex embodies formidable competence. It is sometimes displayed in full view when foreign concerns call in Texas oil men to plug a difficult leak on an underwater well in rough seas. The accumulated competence of petroleum engineers and oil chemists is alive in the pages of the burgeoning special literature, both periodical and monographic. Those who own this kind of expensive investment do not want it to become obsolete.

OPEC, PRICE SWINGS, AND STAGFLATION

Cartel action on petroleum in international trade was predictable, and it came at precisely the moment when the United States began to be vulnerable. U.S. oil imports had represented a minor fraction of total domestic demand through the 1950s and most of the 1960s. In the early 1970s, the quantities imported had risen, rather rapidly, to the extent that a cartel action would be severely felt. When this action came, the consequences for the domestic economy were difficult and appeared unexpectedly hard to understand, even to economists. Paradoxically, U.S. oil companies reaped subsidiary benefits because their profit margins on imported oil applied to much higher prices than before.

The first price action, 1973–1974, raised the price on internationally traded oil several fold. Domestic oil in the United States became subject to price control, which reduced the effect of the price shock on the domestic economy. Price control was also blamed for the inability or unwillingness of the domestic petroleum industry to respond to intensified oil search.

The impact on the U.S. economy (and the economies of several other oil importing countries) was dubbed stagflation because it included a combination of inflation and economic stagnation, an unusual and unexpected situation. Usually, inflation had been associated with economic expansion. If inflation is wage driven, it also leads to rising domestic demand for goods and services because workers will spend their increased wages. Why this did not apply to oil as a source of inflation is not hard to understand, for increased revenues to oil producers do not translate into greatly increased domestic demand for consumer goods—least of all when much of the increased oil revenue goes abroad. This explanation of stagflation was offered shortly afterwards (Dovring 1974) but did not attract much attention.

The OPEC price action of 1973–1974 was followed by a slow downward slide of oil prices in real terms because of continuing inflation, including that let loose by the OPEC price action. As a result there was some adjustment to the new price proportions between oil and other goods, upward adjustment of the prices of other energy sources including coal, natural gas, and electricity, and economic recovery in the mid–1970s.

This phase was followed by a new strong set of price actions on the part of OPEC, with some of its members going farther than the organization had agreed to go. From early 1979 to late 1980, oil prices again increased several fold, and some spot markets registered prices about $40 a barrel. The impact on the United States was magnified by gradual decontrol of the prices of domestic petroleum. Most of this decontrol was accomplished before the end of 1980 (*The Petroleum Situation*). A minor portion had been reserved for decontrol in September 1981 but was actually decontrolled in February of that year, causing the index of oil prices to rise from 680 to 800 or by just under 12 percent.

Again, the sharp rise in petroleum prices caused stagflation, and most economists appeared unable to learn the lesson from the previous round. The same explanation was offered again (Dovring 1981a), pointing to the exceptionally large role automotive fuel plays in the economy of the United States.

Subsequently, real oil prices again decreased because of inflation. Finally, disarray within OPEC in 1986 caused real prices to tumble to their level just after the first oil price action of 1973–1974. This led not only to some degree of recovery in the U.S. economy: it led also to a violent slump in the oil industry, which had difficulty surviving with the international prices of 1974–1975. One result was a sharp drop in the rate of new finds (mainly stripper wells, from infield drilling, as related above). The total stimulus effect on the United States remained weak in 1987.

A side effect of the fluctuations in the oil markets was felt in the banking system. At the height of the euphoria of high hopes in oil exploration in 1980 and 1981, many oil explorers had contracted loans that they could not pay back. Large numbers of such loans had been sold by local oil-state banks to larger banks, and this caused some difficulties—most extremely in the Continental of Illinois and Seattle First, less so in Chase Manhattan (Singer 1985). The link with petroleum affairs was not well communicated to the public, and these financial losses in major banks were not factored into the cost of oil.

OUTLOOK ON U.S. PRODUCTION AND WORLD SUPPLIES

How fast U.S. domestic supply of oil will decline in the 1990s is subject to varying estimates. The doldrums of 1986 were blamed above all on policy, including OPEC price policy or lack thereof (*Oil and Gas Journal*, Editorial, September 15, 1986). One thing remains certain and agreed to by all experts: U.S. domestic oil supply will decline during the 1990s. The decline appears to have begun in 1987. Demand is expected to go

up somewhat. Import demand will rise, maybe to half or more of domestic demand by the year 2000.

Against this stands the outlook for the petroleum exports from other
countries. Recent export history has been deceptive because several oil
exporting countries have been driven by short-term financial needs to
export all they could even at falling prices, even to the point of breaking
the OPEC's hold on prices. But this can not continue. As the years pass,
one after another of the present oil exporting countries will notice two
things: they have less oil left in the ground and they have higher domestic
demand for oil because of industrialization financed by oil revenues and
because of a concomitant increase of automotive transportation. One
after another of those countries will begin to phase out its oil exports
and eventually cease those exports altogether. This crisis in international
petroleum supply should begin about 1990, give or take a year or two.
Ecuador actually served notice several years ago that, failing any large
new oil find in their country, they would begin phasing out oil exports
in 1987 or 1988. Canada and Norway have the same perspective as part
of their long-range oil policy. The likely result, by 2000, is that there
will hardly be any oil exports from countries other than those around
the Persian Gulf. Even the optimistic Conoco estimates are not far from
this scenario (*1984 National Petroleum News Factbook Issue*, pp. 67, 133).

The Persian Gulf is hardly a place that the United States should trust
with half or more of its transportation fuel. Supplies from that area
already now carry heavy overheads in military and political costs. If these
costs were factored into the price of petroleum (which is not done now),
the continued reliance on petroleum as the primary source of transportation fuel would not look as favorable as it is now often made to
appear.

LEGACY OF THE PETROLEUM AGE

Past energy policy in this country has been shortsighted. Leaving it to
market forces made this inevitable, for the individual consumer is as
improvident as a Turkish peasant when it comes to natural resources.
The Turkish peasant who overgrazes his pastures with too many sheep
and goats and so ruins the soil for the future is only as improvident as
he has to be, for his over riding need is that he must eat tomorrow.
When the public in the United States has been just as improvident in
consuming a finite fund resource such as petroleum without making
adequate provisions for replacement fuels, there is no similar excuse.
Individual consumers must shop in the available markets, and the complex of housing and individual transportation is such that most consumers have no choice but to use individual cars for commuting and

shopping, and they live in single-family houses, which have been favored by the tax system (Giertz and Heins 1984).

Policy makers have had more latitude in their choices. And in this country policy makers include many elements of industry. The petroleum industry, the automative complex, the highway system, and the housing interests have made policy by their investment decisions as well as by their lobbying for their interests in federal and state legislatures. In developing the very wasteful systems of housing and transportation that have rendered the U.S. economy the most energy intensive in the world, policy makers yielded step by step to the proddings of business, which wanted to promote social waste for the sake of higher profit levels (Dovring 1984b).

Thus the legacy of the petroleum age in this country is an unusually large national energy budget that is, to a large extent, locked in place by fixed capital in housing and transportation. When the discipline of higher oil prices began to call for "conservation" (that is, more economic use of fuel), the response was tolerably good from manufacturing but much weaker from transportation, which was and remains the most oil dependent sector in the U.S. economy.

Comparisons with other industrialized countries show that the United States spends a much larger share of its national income on housing and transportation than any other country (Dovring 1981a). This in turn is related to the lower rates of savings and the slower rates of economic growth in this country. Again this legacy will be slow to change and will have consequences for a long time to come. Without the extreme reliance on individual automobiles, the United States would have depleted its oil reserves much slower and could have gone on without oil imports for some time. Reckless consumption was compounded by equally reckless disregard for a relatively near-term future. We are not secure even for a decade.

When the systems of housing and transportation are slow to change, it follows that a provident national policy should take in hand the task of redirecting investment by allowing both new and replacement housing to follow less of the common wasteful sprawl. Similarly, the task of redirecting and re-shaping an energy intensive urban transportation system, to make mass transit its mainstay with the individual automobile an auxiliary rather than the leading element, must be part of national policy. But policy induced optimism in the early 1980s even led to a renewed trend toward larger automobiles in the United States. Similarly, as with oil itself, official policy has followed the cues of standard economics to the effect that market forces will correct any imbalances that may occur. How unreasonable this is in regard to housing and transportation should be evident.

The parallel problem of replacing oil itself is much less transparent.

Both politicians and public will need a good deal of new information (or newly organized information) to see that we have no time to lose. The need to provide for replacement fuels is more and more widely recognized in expert comments (Sperhac et al. 1986)

GETTING OUT BEFORE IT IS TOO LATE?

One reason to take the fuel problem in hand much more positively is its increasing uncertainty. Even the business community ought to be sensitive to this. For instance, in attempting to chart oil prices a decade or more into the future, the Department of Energy stated assumptions leading to prices varying as much as 1:2—say, from $45 to $90 by 2000, in 1981 dollars (*Petroleum Economist*, April 1983, citing the National Energy Policy Plan of 1981).

When will it have become too late to escape the commanding lead of petroleum? We seem to get almost as many answers as there are experts. Warnings are already heard even in the engineering press that we are losing precious time (Krieger 1986). It may well be that it is already too late and that some near catastrophic consequences can no longer be avoided. The following will assume, as a matter of reasoning strategy, that a solution can still be found.

One difficulty is in a bewilderingly large array of possible alternatives to petroleum fuels. Against this stands the urgent need to choose a main path of future expansion—a single fuel or a leading one, at least, that will underwrite the energy future of the country, above all in the critical transportation sector. Three problems complicate the arguments of current or immediately prospective costs of producing each of the possible alternative fuels: how capital intensive is each alternative? how long are the lead times for each phase of expansion? and what would be the effects on the economy and on the physical environment, which will be more polluted by some alternative fuels than by others?

3

REPLACING PETROLEUM: THE MANY CHOICES

Sources from which energy goods may be produced fall into two principal categories: minerals and sunshine. Each comes in several forms. Not all of them lend themselves equally well to producing liquid fuel.

The suggestion that energy might to a large and increasing extent be gained from transformed sunshine and that this would represent a "soft" path, which at length would lead to sounder ecology than the "hard" path of mineral energy sources, is not much more than a decade old (Lovins 1976, 1977, 1982). In the planning of the mid–1970s, solar sources as yet played a minor role (*A National Plan* 1976). The complexities of the soft-hard distinction are greater than originally thought (Sperling 1984).

Minerals include coal, oil shale, tar sands, natural gas (some of which may not be fossil), and materials from which nuclear energy can be generated, foremost among them uranium, possibly also deuterium (heavy hydrogen).

Sunshine can be utilized directly for heating by solar collectors and for generating electricity. The largest potential use of solar energy is through biomass or carbohydrates produced through artificial chlorophyll. Wind energy and falling or flowing water also represent transformed sunshine.

Between these two groups of potential sources of energy goods there are some basic differences. Mineral sources are fund resources, subject to being exhausted within some finite time span. Specifically, those reserves of mineral energy sources within reach of economic use are subject to exhaustion within time spans that generally can be specified in decades or in centuries.

Sunshine, by contrast, is a continuing flow. Using today's sunshine will not in any way impair our access to tomorrow's sunshine. Sunshine is also finite in that each day only so much of it falls on the face of the earth. But this quantity is so large that we have little reason to discuss economizing with solar energy.

Mineral sources add heat to the atmosphere when they are used as sources of energy. Even though the heat so generated eventually leaves the atmosphere and goes into outer space, if the additional heat is generated at a sufficiently high rate, it will lead to higher air temperature that may affect the climate. Hydrocarbon fuels also add carbon and generate a "greenhouse effect." This effect causes heat, both the normal solar generated heat and the additional heat generated from mineral sources, to leave the atmosphere at a slower rate. Hence the atmosphere becomes warmer under the greenhouse effect than without this effect. We already have some "heat islands" around large cities. If mineral energy goods are used on a much larger scale than currently, the heating of the atmosphere will be substantial, only to be rendered even more striking to the extent the energy goods are hydrocarbons.

Solar energy goods do not add heat to the atmosphere. The heat that enters the atmosphere is manipulated to supply more concentrated effects in some locations and some functions, but in the end these energy uses decay into heat and reenter the atmosphere in the same amounts that were taken from it by the solar-energy using gadgets or plants. The carbohydrates produced by green plants or by artificial chlorophyll do not add any carbon to the atmosphere. The same carbon that is withdrawn from the air reenters it as the carbohydrates are burned.

Some mineral energy sources also produce pollution on a substantial scale. Apart from much discussed cases of air and water pollution, coal mining often releases sulfuric acid into the ground waters. If coal mining were to be greatly increased, this effect would be magnified. Nuclear energy sources also generate nuclear wastes, the long-term disposal of which is still a problem. All effects on the environment can not be foreseen.

Even conventional air and water pollution will be more expensive to abate, the larger the volume of activity. This is because the larger that volume, the higher the percentage of pollution that must be abated in order to leave the unabated portion within tolerable limits. And it is an elementary tenet of margin theory that the cost of abating 1 percent of the pollution is higher, the closer one comes to 100 percent. At higher levels of activity, the average as well as the marginal cost of abatement will be rising.

Solar energy uses may to some extent generate stresses on the environment. Generally, however, they are minor compared with those from mineral sources.

Because of these and similar differences between the uses of the various sources from which energy goods can be produced, each of these materials must be evaluated regarding secondary or environmental effects as well as conventional costs.

Let us first have an overview of the fossil and nuclear energy sources and then present the case for biomass and artificial chlorophyll.

LIQUID FUELS FROM COAL

Coal is by far the most abundant fossil fuel, if we can trust existing estimates. The quantity data usually published as reserves or resources are not very precise, for two main reasons. One is that to a large extent coal reserves have not yet been found but are inferred from analogous geological conditions. The other is that even if the estimated and inferred quantity of coal in the ground is accurate, not all of it can be extracted and used as fuel.

The nature of coal mining dictates that a good deal of the coal can never be brought up into daylight. Only in open-cast mining (strip mining) can a coal seam be extracted to about 90 percent. Some coal will always be left in the ground even there, in the outskirts of the seam where the coal is mingled with other minerals. In deep mining (underground mining) only about half the coal can be extracted; the other half must be left behind to support the ground above. Trying to extract all the coal would bring down rocks and soil on the miners and would cause the landscape above to cave in.

But that is not all. Most future coal mining will have to be underground; most of the good strip-mining sites have been depleted. But many coal seams cannot be mined at all. Many are down so deep that they could never be mined in open cast; the overburden is too thick. Only very thick seams can allow the stripping of thick overburdens. The German lignite district northeast of Cologne is the extreme case—the world's largest earth-moving enterprise. But in large areas the coal seams are too thin for deep mining. Finally there are many sites where the seam is thick enough for deep mining, but the overburden is too weak. A good deal of the overburden has to be solid rock to allow work under it. To what extent these conditions will allow mining is in many cases not yet known. Mining companies usually investigate these conditions only when they contemplate moving into a new area.

When so much coal has to be left in the ground, the idea has been proposed to burn coal *in situ*, without extracting it. By some ingenious technique the coal may be made to burn underground and the energy recovered by piping it up, as gas or as hot air, to the surface. Technically it is possible, but so far the costs have been discouragingly high. The long-run consequences of reducing underground coal seams to cinders are not clear; the surface could cave in over large areas. Neither is it clear how feasible it might be to contain the fire to designated areas. In Pennsylvania a seam of anthracite (high-quality coal) has been burning out of control for many years, threatening homes and other surface land use.

It is clear in any event that coal might be mined in quantities that would yield far more energy than all the petroleum ever did or could. Hubbert's estimates for coal reserves indicate that coal extraction, if continued and made to respond to the full market demand, would last far into the next century. Unlike petroleum, the quantity of coal is not an immediate concern.

Oil from coal has long been tried. Coking gas used for light and kitchen heat is already an old concept. Germany in the 1930s and early 1940s had numerous small coal conversion plants to make motor fuel for the war machine in World War II. At the time this effort looked big, but, on the scale of the modern industrial world, those plants would not mean much. In a war economy, cost was also no object. In the absence of oil wells of its own, Germany bent on war had to have this supply of synthetic oil at any cost.

At present there is one large enterprise making synthetic oil from coal, the SASOL (South Africa Synthetic Oil) complex in Sasolburgh near Johannesburg. The technology used is basically the same as in wartime Germany, but it has been put in place by U.S. engineers working under contracts that prohibit them from applying exactly the same technological solutions to investments in the United States or elsewhere. Even so, the South African enterprise is also removed from normal market production. The object is to secure transportation fuel in case of an oil embargo that might be designed to make the republic give up some of its national policies.

The notion that the United States might need oil from coal for strategic reasons was discussed in the later 1940s, and a limited program of research and development was initiated. The Paley Commission report in 1952 supported the same. However, the administration coming into office in 1953 disregarded any possibility that synthetic oil might become useful in the United States, and the R & D program that had been started under federal auspices was discontinued. Existing experiment facilities were closed and dismantled. This concerned two installations for oil from coal and one for oil from shale. In the 1950s, the illusion about nuclear-generated electricity becoming "too cheap to meter" contributed to a low regard for coal conversion.

In the 1950s and 1960s, some research on oil from coal was continued by private firms and individual research experts. Sometimes, promising results were announced—prematurely, as it appears. Only after the 1973–1974 oil crisis did oil from coal again appear on the agenda in the

United States in a serious way. At present a large number of research reports are available, and there is no question about the possibility of producing oil and refined oil derivatives from coal. Costs vary from one project to another. Among other things, the accounting of costs is not always comparable from one project to the other. Several projects show that synthetic gasoline could be produced at costs varying from $5 to $19 per million Btu (Herendeen and Dovring 1984, p. 27). One million Btu is the equivalent of eight gallons of standard gasoline, and so the estimates vary from the competitive to the futuristic. At $1 per gallon of gasoline, several processes would be competitive; at $2 per gallon, nearly all of them would be.

The matter is rendered more complex by uncertainty and by insufficient information about actual costs in large-scale operation, none of which currently exists in the United States. The South African SASOL project publishes very little information for the benefit of the rest of the world. One indicator might be the reluctance of U.S. oil companies to invest in coal-to-oil plants, but this again might be influenced by their industrial strategy, which calls for maintaining petroleum as the leading fuel as long as possible.

Cost estimates on a pilot scale might not be the whole answer. Coal liquefaction requires both access to coal in large quantities and access to other resources and facilities, foremost among them water. How many coal-to-oil plants of a given capacity could be built in a given area, regarding water and other limiting factors? For one state, Illinois, the answer from a rather conservative set of assumptions is that the state could build enough plants to fill its own needs for transportation fuel and also for exporting half that amount (one-third of prospective production) to other states (Herendeen and Dovring 1984, p. 7).

This result does not by any means indicate whether the whole road fleet in the United States could be fueled by oil derived from coal. Illinois is not only one of the most coal rich states in the country; it is also rare in combining its coal riches with abundant sweet water. Western states with large coal deposits, often of higher quality from the viewpoint of both direct burning and processing into oil, are less well endowed with available water. Ingenious projects have been designed for transporting finely ground coal by slurry pipelines or for piping water into the coal areas from afar. All this would serve only to increase the total costs of utilizing coal for liquid fuel on a large scale.

None of this explains how far we could tolerate the pollution of air and water generated by greatly stepped-up use of coal. Nor does it meet the general problem of greenhouse effect in the atmosphere.

In between, there is a possible interim solution of coal refining. Coal need not necessarily be made into gasoline. It could also be used to produce methanol. This would be a simpler industrial process. Most of the coal refining proceeds by way of methane or other gasification, and from gas to methanol the step is simpler than from gas to gasoline. If a long-run policy aims to replace gasoline and diesel fuel with methanol as road fuel, methanol from coal could be a stopgap until the biomass sources have been developed sufficiently to supply all road fuel.

In the early 1980s, the cost of producing methanol from coal was much lower than in the case of biomass feedstocks. An estimate deriving from a 1982 report (Goodrich 1983, p. 8) indicates methanol from coal as the cheapest of the synthetic fuels. It was also cheaper than gasoline when the crude oil price was $32.50 as in 1980, a condition that may well be repeated in the 1990s if no sooner. Cost estimates made close to the petroleum industry represent methanol from coal as considerably more expensive than gasoline (Cohen and Muller 1984).

Methanol from coal has also been the focus of attempts to promote methanol by federal legislation (U.S. Congress 1984; U.S. Congress 1986a). House Resolution 3355 was approved by the House in October 1986 but not by the Senate before the 99th Congress adjourned.

LIQUID FUELS FROM NATURAL GAS

Synthetic fuels based on natural gas are the simplest to produce. Nearly all the methanol produced in the United States at present has natural gas as the raw material. So far, this has appeared to be the cheapest source of methanol. Various proposals have also been made to produce gasoline from natural gas, as a means of prolonging the use of this type of liquid fuel and of postponing the transition to new types and sources of fuel.

The weakness of such proposals is often emphasized by experts working for the oil interests: natural gas is itself a scarce natural resource. It is already a high-grade fuel, and it is most logical to use it in gaseous form for the purposes for which it is currently used. In some areas where natural gas is abundant, it is used also to generate electricity.

The logic is clear enough. As long as natural gas remains limited, as at present, large-scale conversion to liquid fuels appears inadvisable. This does not preclude some use of natural gas-based methanol (along with coal-based supply) in the initial phase of a transition to methanol fueled cars, before biomass-based supplies have been built up in sufficient quantity. Current experiments with methanol powered automobiles (mainly in California) use methanol produced mainly from natural gas. The same source also enters the current limited use of methanol in gasoline blends ("gasohol").

In the event that primal gas were to be discovered in very large quantities, we would have to consider the environmental damage from overheating and the greenhouse effect.

OIL FROM SHALE AND TAR SANDS

Oil shale and tar sands represent some of the geological formations from which a good deal of petroleum was formed in past geological epochs. In their solid or semisolid form, they present greater difficulty of extraction than does liquid petroleum in underground pools or porous rocks.

Oil shale is available in large quantities in Wyoming and some adjacent states. There are also shale deposits of a different character (and usually of lower oil content) elsewhere, such as in the lower Appalachians and the Ozark hills. The total amount of oil in shale in the United States is estimated to be larger than total world oil reserves. It may even exceed the energy content in U.S. coal reserves (Griskey 1986). The same objections as to coal and primal gas will then apply.

Tar sands are known in many places, but the largest quantities (or, at least, those most talked about) are in Alberta, Canada. The total oil potential in tar sands is not as large as that in shales, but it is still impressive (Griskey 1986).

Oil shale is sometimes used as a solid fuel in small local kilns for lime production. Larger applications of shale as solid fuel are in Soviet Estonia and in Israel, both areas where costs and returns are not watched as carefully as in most market economy countries. In the United States, shale as solid fuel is not considered a viable alternative to coal.

Attempts to produce oil from shale date at least from the early synthetic-fuel experiments about 1950. One such installation was among those scrapped in or shortly after 1953. Oil shale was given renewed attention in 1973, and some pilot-scale production exists. Repeated departures toward larger investments have been canceled again and again.

The problem is twofold: unit cost and the call on other resources, foremost water. The problem with cost is to factor in the price of input energy at each prospective price level of output energy. A study from the late 1970s seemed to show that shale oil would become economically viable whenever the price of crude oil would rise to $18 a barrel (Ericsson and Morgan 1978). If that had been realistic, shale oil should have had excellent prospects in 1979 and would have remained in that position except for a short time in 1986–1987 when OPEC disarray sent crude oil prices lower. Yet no such conclusion came from the oil industry. The difficulty with the 1978 study is that it varied the price of the output but not the prices of the inputs, some of which are energy goods or other energy-intensive goods. Thus the higher price of crude oil would automatically lead to higher costs, so the output price needed to pay for the operation would always be higher than it seemed in the static analysis of the study.

Apart from such uncertainties, the oil industry also has had its sight on the conditions for large-scale operation. The most conventional technique for extracting oil from shale requires large quantities of water, which is not easy to get in those mountain areas. The water in the rivers of the region is generally claimed for other and more immediate concerns, many of them downstream. Other techniques, such as *in situ* recovery through injection of burning gas at high temperatures into canals drilled in the rocks, are energy intensive so that the net payoff in available energy is low compared to gross output. Such techniques also tend to become more difficult to handle on a large scale than on a pilot scale. The net result is that the oil industry refused large-scale commitments.

Some of the same problems also attend the extraction of oil from tar sands such as those in Canada. Some quantity may be extactible at remunerative costs, but the quantity is limited by water and by other practicalities of the operations. No very large annual contribution to the fuel supply of the world, or of the United States, can be expected from this source.

NUCLEAR POWER

Electricity from nuclear reactors was once hailed as the great shining hope for the later twentieth century. From being seen as "too cheap to meter" in the 1950s, nuclear electricity has become less and less plausible and, in any event, more expensive than electricity from coal-fired generators. Between the twin obstacles of rising costs and unacceptable hazards, the future of nuclear-generated electricity is now seriously in doubt. This is so even without considering the large and hard-to-calculate overheads of security from radioactive waste products and security from theft and sabotage. The least likely part of a nuclear future is that nuclear power could also let us produce liquid motor fuel cheaper than by other means.

Nuclear power comes in several varieties. Some are already functioning on a sizable scale, others mainly on a pilot scale. Some are still merely laboratory experiments. The principal alternatives, as known to the public, are fission of naturally fissionable uranium, fission of plutonium bred from nonfissionable uranium, fission of a rare uranium isotope bred in quantity from thorium, and fusion of deuterium (heavy hydrogen) nuclei—the H-bomb principle.

The current generation of nuclear power stations uses reactors to generate electricity by steam pressure powered by fission of naturally fissionable uranium, U^{235}. Such uranium is a small fraction (less than 1 percent) of the uranium occurring in nature. Most of the uranium in nature is a heavy isotope that is not naturally fissionable but has some technical uses such as in radiation shields and armor-breaking ammunition. To be usable in fission reactors, the uranium extracted from rocks is enriched until it holds about 3 percent U^{235}. After most of the fissionable uranium has been used up, there remains in the spent fuel rods a mixture of some unspent U^{235}, some unchanged heavy uranium, some plutonium generated from the heavy uranium through the processes of the reactors, and debris of uranium (and plutonium) nuclei, which were split in the fission process.

These fission fragments are lighter elements, to a large extent radioactive. The two most important are radioactive caesium and radioactive strontium, both with half lives of some decades and continued radioactive hazards for centuries. Such fission fragments have to be stored somewhere out of harm's way. For the most part, the contents of spent fuel rods are now kept in temporary storage on the premises of the nuclear power stations. To some extent, they are also used in conventional power stations (coal-fired ones, for instance) where the heat generated by the radioactive fission fragments can help deliver the initial warming of boiler water. Only recently have places of intended permanent storage begun to be designated and equipped in this country.

Instead of burying the contents of the spent fuel rods as they leave the reactors, the fission fragments can also be sorted out by a process which separates the usable elements: the unspent uranium, both fissionable and nonfissionable, and the plutonium. The latter is also usable as fission fuel, in fact some was used within the old fuel rods as it was produced. Plutonium is above all the explosive material in many nuclear weapons. Recovering it from spent fuel rods presents the danger of theft for purpose of blackmail or sabotage. The process of separating the elements is expensive, however, and it is not clear whether this is the best way to obtain more fuel for power stations.

Fissionable uranium was long thought to be relatively scarce. With mechanical means of extraction, crushing the rocks into small fragments, costs were acceptable when the metal occurred in concentrations from 3,000 parts per million (0.3 percent) to 500 parts per million (0.05 percent). Lower concentrations were thought uneconomical. There are very large amounts of low-grade uranium ores (such as 30 parts per million, 0.003 percent) in deposits such as the Chattanooga shales in Tennessee. By mechanical extraction, fissionable uranium was thought to be so scarce that this source of energy, at present levels of use, would disappear in a few decades. Now uranium can be extracted by other means such as leaching from the rocks without as much crushing as before. This lowers the cost and renders lower-grade deposits eligible for extraction. Hence, the possible scope of the conventional uranium reactor is correspondingly larger, difficult to say by how much.

Even so, the costs of conventional uranium reactors are high. High construction costs in this country may in some cases be due to incidental mismanagement, but on the whole they reflect the higher safety standards imposed following experience with existing reactors. There have been more near-catastrophic episodes than the public knows. These lead to more down time, which takes away some of the operational advantage that nuclear power stations should have over those fired by fossil fuels. The essential lesson of Three Mile Island is that a nuclear power station is a place where you can lose a billion dollars in half an hour. The lesson from Chernobyl is that a simple mishap can lay waste towns and countryside over hundreds of square miles, apart from spreading radioactive fallout over many countries. Forestalling such accidents will only render fission generating power stations more expensive.

Even with the cheaper means of extracting uranium from rocks, it is doubtful that nuclear power can become the mainstay of energy supply unless the raw material source is even larger. This is what the breeder reactors seemed to promise: uranium to plutonium or thorium to uranium.

The plutonium breeder reactor manufactures plutonium (Pu^{239}) from heavy nonfissionable uranium (U^{238}), which is 99 percent of the uranium in nature. It does so at a higher rate than it consumes fuel, whether U^{235} or plutonium, in its own operation. Thus, each cycle of production leaves the power station with more fuel than it had at the beginning. The breeder proportion is about 1.33:1. Consequently, three breeder reactors burning U^{235} could supply plutonium to four other reactors, whether they are breeders or not. When the fissionable uranium is depleted and the breeder reactors burn plutonium, three breeders could supply fuel to themselves and a fourth one, which need not be a breeder. All told, the fuel base for nuclear electricity generation could be multiplied by a larger number—say, by a factor of 50. The plutonium breeder could last us for several centuries.

The costs are another matter, even without counting the contribution to overheating the atmosphere. That kind of consequence would be less severe than the greenhouse effect of unlimited fossil hydrocarbon fuels, but the heating from very large numbers of reactors might be severe even so.

Cost calculations made in this country indicate that breeders would cost about twice as much to build as do conventional fission plants. Operational costs are even less predictable. In the whole world there are now three full-scale breeder power stations. Two of these are in the Soviet Union, and their cost data would at best be hard to analyze even if we had access to them. The third is in France and was commissioned recently, so there are at best preliminary cost calculations based on short experience.

Whatever the conventional costs of breeder power stations, the costs for security would be very large if the system were built to supply a mainstay of the energy system. A chain is only as strong as its weakest link, and the longer the chain, the more weak links there are certain to be. The need for security would grow exponentially with the size of the system, for even one major theft of plutonium would raise unacceptably high hazards for terrorist action. The quality of security personnel would decrease as the size of the system increased, and this would necessitate even more security checks, of this personnel and of their relatives and friends. In the end we would have a complete police state, and that is too high a price to pay for electricity. To compound it, if a large nuclear power system were built, we would all be hostage to it, for the alternatives would no longer be viable. A large system cannot be abandoned and replaced in short order, and expertise for other systems would not have thrived in the shadow of a mainstay nuclear power system.

The other kind of breeder reactor is designed to breed light uranium, U^{233}, from thorium, Th^{232}. Light uranium is very scarce in nature, but thorium is reasonably plentiful, so a large nuclear-power system might be built around this concept. A pilot-scale plant (80 megawatts) was commissioned in the late 1970s, at Shippingport, a Pennsylvania town not far from Pittsburgh. Not much has been heard about experience gained from this plant. In any event, it appears that the breeder proportion would be less than 1, so the increment in fuel supply would not be as large as from the plutonium breeder.

Finally there is the concept of fusion energy, or the H-bomb principle. Theoretically it might work. The raw material is deuterium (D^2) or heavy hydrogen. It occurs in all the water on earth, and the whole quantity of it, if used for fusion energy, might see us through a couple of millennia. The objections as to overheating the atmosphere would be the same as those to plutonium breeders. But the technical problems are so staggering that there seems to be no viable solution in sight. The problem of manipulating a glowing blob of gas at several million degrees temperature can be handled by one or another device keeping the blob or plasm suspended in midair, but even then the suspension mechanisms have to be controlled by some surrounding structure. Even when this structure is far enough from the glowing gas not to be overheated by it, the structure keeps being prematurely ruined by radiation from wayward particles originating in the glowing gas. There are not even any beginning guesses concerning costs, so it is not reasonable to expect fusion energy to become a viable power source soon in our economy.

All the above might be enough to put the nuclear energy alternatives to rest. We should, however, also consider the problems of transmuting electricity into motive power for vehicles. Electric car motors have been no great success, and the main focus of a search for nuclear-generated car fuel has been by way of liquid or gaseous fuels. Hydrogen gas could be produced by electrolysis from water if the current were cheap enough (which it is not). But hydrogen gas is far too volatile to be placed in the hands of ordinary motorists. It might be delivered in some other form, such as metal hydrides from which the gas would be released as needed. This obviously would only add further to the already high costs of nuclear energy. Therefore we have no reason to expect that a mainstay of automotive transportation fuel will come to us from nuclear processes.

SOLAR ELECTRICITY

As late as 1976, official policy debate made very little of solar energy as a possible power source. The 1976 plan (*A National Plan* 1976) stresses nuclear power but limits discussion of solar energy to direct heating and cooling and to electricity by thermal and photovoltaic techniques and by windmills.

Hydropower, the largest element of solar energy producing electricity, is already in place. This is a substantial yet limited part of the energy system of the United States. Some small countries such as Norway and Switzerland draw a much larger part of their energy needs from hydropower, and the same may become true of some other countries such as Egypt, Nepal, and Zaire. In the United States most of the waterfalls that can produce hydroelectricity are already doing so. Electricity could also be produced, at higher costs, from power stations on rivers with swift stream flow without forming water falls. The size of this potential appears not to have been explored.

Windmills would obviously be limited in scope and to small-scale units, which could be practical on the local scene. Thermal and photovoltaic techniques still are far from being competitive with conventional sources of electricity.

In any event, the further step of producing liquid or gaseous fuels by means of electricity would carry with it the same added costs as in the case of electricity from nuclear power sources. It would hardly belong in the perspective for quite some time.

BIOMASS

The 1976 plan did not even mention biomass, but a few years later there was increased use of wood as fuel replacing coal or oil. The wood-using industries (sawmills and pulpmills) are increasingly burning their own waste wood such as sawdust, bark, and leftover wood fragments as industrial fuel. Wood returned as household fuel to forest rich areas with cold winters such as northern New England.

Burning wood is obviously a minor part of the possible uses for biomass because, among other things, wood burners necessitate more upkeep than heating devices using more efficient fuels. The penalty for neglect is increased fire hazard. The bulk of biomass energy possibilities is instead in the refining of crops, crop refuse, hay, wood, and garbage into liquid and gaseous fuels.

Current estimates·of biomass energy potential in the United States often indicate only a very limited place for biomass in the future energy system of the country. One recent assessment ("Biomass energy" 1983) concluded that total annual gross biomass energy formation in the United States was less than total energy use in the country and that other uses such as food and timber, and conversion losses, would leave only about 5 percent of the annual energy budget of the country to come from biomass.

Such estimates overlook several things. One is that their estimates reflect average actual production rather than potential production from higher yielding strains of grasses and trees. Another is that both domestic food demand and export demand for agricultural products may change with higher energy prices. Yet another is that current energy use in this country is in many ways wasteful and that a more rational energy system would need a smaller total energy budget. Finally, biomass will not be called upon to supply all energy needs. Eventually, other forms of solar energy will also become important.

The late 1970s saw a great upsurge of interest in and activity on biomass-based fuels. "Gasohol" (a 90:10 blend of gasoline and ethyl alcohol) was already much talked about and to some extent used in 1978. It was an important part of the rationale for subsequent research in the U.S. Department of Energy. In 1979, the DOE set forth calculations of the amounts of biomass-based ethanol and methanol that could be produced up to the year 2000 (USDOE, *The Report of the Alcohol Fuels Policy Review*, 1979). According to this report, biomass could yield as much as 54 billion gallons of ethanol or, alternatively 12 billion gallons of ethanol and 155 billion gallons of methanol. The latter alternative assumes that wood, agricultural residues, and municipal solid waste (MSW) are used to produce methanol instead of ethanol. The former alternative would represent about 10 percent of annual gasoline consumption in this country, the latter over 40 percent. Evidently, biomass was already recognized as a major potential source, mainly because of the methanol alternative. Even so, methanol was assumed to come mainly from wood and secondarily from agricultural residues, with MSW as a minor source.

These estimates are on the conservative side, especially so for methanol. How much higher the production potential may be or may become will be explored in later chapters.

At about the same time, the Office of Technology Assessment (OTA) published parallel sets of estimates (U.S. Congress, *Energy from Biological Processes*, 1980). The conversion factors are different from those in the DOE report. Among other things, the yield of liquid fuel from wood and grass is assumed to be nearly the same with ethanol as with methanol.

This assumption is clearly at variance with the DOE calculations as well as with most subsequent ones. On such assumptions, the OTA found a possible contribution of biomass for all purposes of about 20 percent of the national energy budget, with a similar percentage of motor fuel.

Since 1979–1980 there has been a great deal of new research on production of feedstocks and on costs and conversion rates. The economic perspectives for food farming have also changed since the export expansion of the mid–1970s. The following chapters will bring the picture closer to date and present it in more detail.

Even when only ethanol and methanol are considered, opinions about what can be accomplished have varied widely. As late as 1984, the Organization for Economic Cooperation and Development (OECD) in Paris published a report on biomass energy (*Biomass for Energy*, 1984) that was extremely timid in its assumptions. It discounts methanol because of technical problems that were already being handled with some success. It also disregards any future changes in diets and food technology.

On much the same lines, the USDA report of 1983 (USDA, *A Biomass Energy Production and Use Plan*, 1983) also concentrates on ethanol for gasohol blends, assuming that current market forces should be a sufficient guide for the future. This was in accordance with administration policy then in effect, but it is unrealistic for long-range planning.

Outside official policy debate, private research scholars have made much larger projections for the use of synthetic fuels, both biomass based and others. Methanol could fuel about half the automobile fleet by the year 2000 (Goodrich 1983). Most of this would come from coal, but both methanol and ethanol from biomass are treated as feasible alternatives. Another fuel perspective discusses the option of producing biomass fuel where we now grow livestock feed, in which case ethanol could fill a large part of the future fuel bill (Mitchell et al. 1983).

Apart from the two main alternatives for biomass-based liquid fuels, some other alternatives are debated. Alcohols could also be produced from some minor sources such as citrus rinds, cheese whey, and other agricultural processing wastes (Guymont and Alpert, 1978). Butanol (butyl alcohol, a heavy alcohol) has also been discussed as a possible liquid fuel, mainly in mixtures with other fuels (Noon 1980). Several attempts have been made to show that vegetable oils could be used as propulsion fuel. Sunflower oil was proposed in South Africa (Bruwer et al. 1981). Rapeseed oil has been investigated in West Germany (Buhner and Kogl 1981). Closer to home, soybean oil has repeatedly been proposed, again because of concerns for creating more outlets for U.S. farm products. It appears that the price of gasoline should approach $2 a gallon before such an edible vegetable oil could compete. The yield per area unit would also be low.

In the following, interest will focus on the principal alcohol fuels. Ethanol will be treated in Chapter 4; methanol, in all the following ones.

ARTIFICIAL CHLOROPHYLL

The production of carbohydrate chemicals by means of artificial chlorophyll now appears to be a technological fact (Rebeiz et al. 1983). Whenever this may be expanded to field-scale production, feedstock for all U.S. energy needs might be produced from a small fraction of the country's area equivalent to the state of Arizona. Whenever this comes of age in the sense of producing at lower cost than other energy sources, the entire situation will be changed radically for the better. Concerns for resource limitations may be a thing of the past or the very remote future. To date we have no indication, however, when or even whether carbohydrates from artificial chlorophyll will become an economically viable alternative.

4

GASOHOL—A BLIND ALLEY

Alcohol from grain is a very old concept. For centuries, a large part of the market for strong alcoholic beverages has been met by products obtained from fermentation of grain-derived sugars, which in turn were obtained from grain starch by various prefermentation treatments.

Grain alcohol has at times served as a stabilizer on the supply and prices of grains. This has been implicit since grain alcohol gained substantial volume. Sometimes it was made explicit by legislation. The conversion of grain into beverages might be prohibited in years of short crops when the grain price would be high in any event. It was left unhampered in years of large grain supplies and low prices.

High-grade alcohol keeps indefinitely; there is no loss in storage. Carry-over stocks of beverage alcohol could render some of the same services that we associate with the Commodity Credit Corporation, federal farm supports, and the "ever normal granary." Even for fuel alcohol, the unlimited storage time is an advantage over gasoline, which will deteriorate if stored more than a few months.

Fuel alcohol has not been entirely unknown, but until recently it had very limited practical applications such as in spirit lamps (etnas). It took an unusual combination of high oil prices and falling grain prices to initiate large-scale fuel use for grain alcohol.

A SUPPLY DRIVEN INITIATIVE

There is no doubt that the gasohol initiative of the late 1970s reflected above all the farm interest in developing new uses for grains, especially corn. Politicians declaring themselves "gasoholics" were typically from

Corn Belt states. Uppermost in the early debate was the extent to which grain could be withdrawn from the conventional grain markets by a demand for fuel alcohol. Tempering this was the repeated question whether uses of grain for fuel alcohol might reach such proportions that food prices could be raised as a consequence.

Only in a subsequent phase of the debate did it begin to be evident that large-scale use of fuel alcohol from grains might damage the soils by expansion of row crops over land vulnerable to erosion or by withdrawal of crop residues to serve as feedstock for ethyl alcohol. The former concerns were not the farmers' in the first round of debate. The 1970s had seen a good deal of tilling of conservation land, including many of the grassy waterways that had been established to moderate the flow of abundant surface water from melting snow or from violent rainstorms. The concept for many farmers (and some of their advisors) was "hedgerow to hedgerow corn," with no treelines or other windbreaks. When that expansive drive was frustrated by falling grain prices in the late 1970s, the scene appeared ready for the gasohol initiative.

THE EARLY PRODUCTION TARGETS

From the start it was evident that ethyl alcohol from crops would become an additive, not a "neat" fuel. Gasoline-powered car engines cannot use unblended alcohol without extensive modification. The engine thus modified, in turn, can no longer use unblended gasoline. Under U.S. conditions, it was decided early that the acceptable proportion would be 10 percent ethyl alcohol to 90 percent gasoline. This blend is supposed not to harm the gasoline-burning engine. In South America, some countries accept 20 percent ethyl alcohol in their gasoline blends.

The percentages relate to possible supply sources. In South America, Brazil and some other countries have large supplies—actual or potential—of sugar cane, a feedstock that allows the simplest possible path of conversion into ethyl alcohol. In the United States, sugar cane and other sucrose-producing crops such as sweet sorghum represent a much smaller potential. Instead, the possible supply of fuel alcohol would have to come principally from the starch in grain and from other crops such as potatoes, which are an old source of beverage alcohol. Ethyl alcohol can also be obtained from cellulose materials such as wood and crop residues, but with these the constraints are more severe.

In 1978 when the Department of Energy set the production target to obtain ethyl alcohol at the volume of 10 percent of the gasoline used in the country, it clearly recognized that such a role for fuel alcohol would remain subsidiary; the new fuel would not be a mainstay or stand-alone energy good. This conclusion could only be strengthened by the prevailing opinion that gasohol would need tax subsidies to be viable, even when gasoline prices were considerably higher than in the base case (David et al. 1978).

There has also been some use of methanol as a component in gasohol blends, but there have been difficult technical problems with these blends, and consumer dissatisfaction with such blends has sometimes called the entire gasohol concept into question.

PRODUCTION PATHS FOR ETHANOL

There are three principal paths of producing ethyl alcohol from bio-mass materials. They all include fermentation by yeast and distillation by the application of heat. The production paths have different lengths and different alcohol yields depending on whether the feedstock is a sugar crop, a starchy crop, or some cellulose material.

Producing alcohol from sugar crops such as sugar cane or sweet sorghum is the simplest of the three paths. Where the feedstock crops are high yielding, they also yield the most alcohol per unit of land used to grow feedstock. In the case of sugar cane, however, there is an illusion; it is often overlooked that the high yields per area unit are gained by using the land twelve months of the year just for sugar cane. This is in tropical or subtropical climates where the alternative land uses might include two or more crops a year.

The sugar crops are treated mechanically to extract the sugary sap, a raw sucrose. Sugar cane and sweet sorghum are run through a simple crusher. With sugar beets, a somewhat more complicated procedure is needed. Unlike sugar production for food, the sucrose from the sugar crops need not be refined when the target product is fuel alcohol.

The sucrose liquid is placed in a fermentation tank where it is con-verted into low-grade alcohol (hydrous alcohol, a beerlike fluid). This alcohol contains too much water to be used as fuel. Most if not all of the water must be removed by running the product through a distillation column. The more completely the water is removed, the more expensive the alcohol. The last few percentage points are the most expensive to remove. For use in gasoline blends, the alcohol must be totally free from water or anhydrous (100 percent or 200 proof). For use alone, as neat fuel, alcohol can contain some 10 percent water or even more depending on the type of engine. Such mildly hydrous alcohol may even have a somewhat better effect because of steam pressure.

Thus, the use in gasohol causes a higher unit cost for ethanol than its use in neat fuel. This extends to the production from starch or cellulose. The fermentation and distillation phases are essentially the same with all three types of feedstock.

When the feedstock is sugar cane, the crushed cane or "bagasse" is usually burned in the cane sugar mills for process heat. This minimizes handling costs of the bulky residual.

Ethyl alcohol from starchy crops such as grains and tubers requires a longer path of production. Before fermentation, the starch must be converted to sugar. The ground or mashed feedstock undergoes an enzyme treatment in a special tank. The complete installation for grain alcohol production thus includes a whole series of fixed gadgets of considerable volume. The production also takes longer than that for sugary feedstocks. All of this has consequences for costs of production—the costs of obtaining, installing, and maintaining the fixed equipment and of manpower engaged in the operation. The enzyme materials are also an added cost.

The yield of alcohol fuel can be as high as 2.5 gallons of ethanol per bushel of corn. A bushel of corn weighs 56 pounds or about 25 kilograms. A corn yield of 100 bushels an acre would mean 250 gallons of ethanol an acre, or about 2,400 liters a hectare. 100 bushels an acre is below current average corn yield in the United States.

Unlike the sugar crop alternatives and the cellulose feedstock alternatives, the starchy sources leave behind considerable amounts of feed grade proteins, which constitute a joint product of substantial value. All three methods release carbon dioxide, which can be used in several technical applications such as enriching the atmosphere in greenhouses, as an ingredient in carbonated soft drinks, or as a lubricant in tertiary oil extraction.

Using cellulose as feedstock is both costlier and more problematic than using starchy crops. In order to turn the cellulose into starch, yet one more step of conversion is needed, performed by another set of enzymes in another set of tanks. There are further complications when the cellulose (as is often the case) is associated with lignin. The total yield of ethanol per unit of feedstock is much lower than with starchy feedstock. The yield is also much lower than in the case of methanol from cellulose. Much research is being done on increasing the yield of ethanol from such feedstocks.

COSTS OF ETHANOL FROM GRAIN

New products are more complicated to evaluate than old ones because we have less experience with complex market reactions. Grain alcohol is far from being new, but fuel alcohol poses some problems different from those of beverage or even industrial alcohol because the different use imposes different cost constraints and some difference in applied technology.

Let us distinguish costs from overhead effects. There are costs in money and costs in energy both direct and indirect, which become relevant when the intended product is an energy good. There are also repercussion effects when resources begin to be drawn upon in quantity for a new use. Fuel alcohol has the potential to be produced in far greater quantities than either beverage or industrial alcohol. Further there are effects on the environment, both the narrow one of land use and its capability and the wider one of air and water quality.

Money cost is not so simple a concept as it may sound. There are problems of applied technology, which are not the same for large and small production units. There are also intricate bookkeeping problems when the same process yields more than one product, as is the case with alcohol from grain.

The policy signals of the later 1970s included some tax breaks. The new departure led to a rash of interest in building small-scale alcohol plants, on or near farms, designed to take advantage of the special savings possible at the farm level. Elaborate instructions were written to help small-scale investors (Chambers 1979; *Fuel from Farms* 1980; *Fuel Alcohol on the Farm* 1980). Tax advantages in many states were designed to place alcohol production from grain within reach of many new entrepreneurs. In the state of Illinois alone, there were at one time in 1980 over 100 applications for licenses to build alcohol plants, which had to be licensed by the federal Bureau of Alcohol, Tobacco, and Firearms. Safeguards had to be arranged to prevent fuel alcohol from being diverted to beverage use.

There were some cost advantages on paper, and in the absence of technical complications, the farm-fuel distillery ought to have made economic sense (Dovring et al. 1980). The technical complications turned out to be many, ranging from faulty equipment bought at apparent bargain prices from fly-by-night firms, to intricacies of alcohol chemistry and the retrieval of sieve materials (Herendeen and Reidenbach 1982). In the end, not much came of the drive for on-farm distilleries.

Grain alcohol comes now almost entirely from large industrial producers who can take full advantage of all byproducts, including carbon dioxide, used in greenhouses, and heavy alcohols such as butanol and propanol, which have industrial uses. Such large processors also incur the maximum of those costs that on-farm distilleries can reduce: the large firm pays the full market price for grain and must dry the feed residue to storage standards and to be sold at wholesale prices.

To calculate the money cost of alcohol in such industrial plants would be difficult in the best of circumstances, which should include full access to the firm's accounting system. Joint products can be priced differently depending on industrial policy set by the firm.

Some of the alcohol going into gasohol is produced by plants owned or controlled by oil distributors who want to secure their own supply. This complicates the question of cost because alcohol serves as an octane booster. Other means of raising the octane imply further processing steps, which cost more than the alcohol. This includes the energy cost of refining to higher octane ratings. This cost may be higher than the added energy costs of supplying the alcohol. Some oil distributors are against the gasohol concept because it reduces the primary demand for petroleum products.

The gasohol concept has penetrated the gasoline market very incompletely. Use of methanol in some blends points to insufficient domestic supply of ethanol at acceptable prices. So do the imports of fuel ethanol from Brazil.

Parallel with the money cost runs the energy cost, which is always high for ethyl alcohol and higher with grain than with most other feedstocks. To the energy cost of grinding or crushing, enzyme treatment, fermentation, and distillation are added those of growing the crops (Chambers et al. 1979). This problem is particularly puzzling in the case of corn, which uses up much nitrogen fertilizer. That the corn plant uses the nitrogen to build protein, a substance not used to produce alcohol, does not help the accounting problem. Again, the energy balance as against other protein sources must be considered by itself.

LOGISTICS OF GRAIN ALCOHOL

Calculating the costs of producing fuel alcohol from grain based on present prices of grain and other inputs would be fallacious. A large new activity has its own repercussion effects on the markets from which supplies are to be drawn. Displacing large amounts of corn into alcohol production would be sure to raise the price of corn, thus increasing both food prices and the money cost of alcohol fuel. Vigorous expansion would thus be choked off unless subsidies are very large. In real terms, rising grain prices would elicit more grain production, which would mean rising costs at the margin. Raising the yields of lands already producing corn would necessitate larger expenses for fertilizers and other inputs—larger at the margin than in the average. Expanding corn production to lands not now used for corn would also raise the average cost of production in both money and materials. Increasing the amount of row cropping would exacerbate soil erosion on sloping or otherwise vulnerable lands and lead to increased overhead costs.

These are some of the reasons why the production target for grain alcohol of covering 10 percent of the road fuel demand is an ambitious target. Reaching it would require that other sources besides grain be added to the alcohol production potential.

Another part of the logistics of large-scale grain alcohol production concerns the use of byproducts. Some of these could outproduce their markets. This includes the CO_2 for greenhouse use; how much greenhouse produce can one sell? Capturing the carbon dioxide for other uses is costlier than piping it to a nearby greenhouse. Another group of byproducts are the heavy alcohols (sometimes called fusel oils) for which there are industrial uses but within low quantitative limits. Fuel use of butanol is at least problematic (Noon 1980).

High-grade protein feed, an important output of alcohol fermentation especially from grain, is a byproduct that could displace its market. Not only is the protein in the grain not used up, the fermentation bacteria improve its quality. Under the name DDG (distillers' dry grain), this distillery product is a valuable component in many mixed livestock feeds. Sometimes DDGS is recognized separately (the S stands for soluble ingredients that are sometimes included in the distillery residue). The precise manner in which DDG or DDGS is mixed with other feeds, and what kinds of livestock these are fed to, also influences the feed value and hence the economic value to the livestock producers. If large amounts of corn are converted to alcohol and DDG, other high-grade stockfeeds such as soybean meal might be displaced. Soybeans are produced with less energy input than corn, and expansion of corn production at the expense of soybeans will therefore mean more energy intensive farming. The proposal to use soybean oil as liquid motor fuel would lead to even more soybean meal coming on the markets; soybean oil and gasohol would not be compatible within the same energy system.

The proposal has been made to supplement DDG with lower-grade cellulose feeds (to cattle and sheep), thus replacing whole corn rather than soybeans and lessening the increase in corn production and acreage that would normally follow from fuel alcohol being produced from corn (Herman 1981b). This would require that large numbers of livestock producers adopt and learn to use the complicated new feed mixes. Implicitly the proposal assumes that the actual production of ethanol from grain will remain far below the maximum target of 10 percent of the road fuel.

COSTS AND LOGISTICS OF ETHANOL FROM CELLULOSE FEEDSTOCKS

As described above, producing ethanol from cellulose feedstocks takes longer and requires more fixed installations than producing ethanol from starchy materials. Thus capital and labor costs must be higher, too. This will partially offset the lower unit cost of the feedstock. The fermentation residual is also not as valuable as that from grains. At the same time the ultimate fuel yield from cellulose feedstocks is also much lower than that from grains. This yield contributes further to offsetting the lower feedstock price.

Compounding all of this are the logistics of supplying and storing the cellulose feedstocks. Unlike methanol, which may be produced in small mobile units, the ethanol-from-cellulose plants have to be large and immobile. Given the low fuel yield, feedstocks need to be supplied in large physical quantities—great bulk and weight. Because biomass feedstocks are produced over vast areas, the supply area for even a moderate-sized plant would have to be large. Costs of transportation would be high for any kind of biomass feedstock. Wood might be stored where it is felled and trucked in continuously during the operation of the ethanol plant. Dry crop materials (whether residues or hay) would have to be stored at the plant during much of the year. Some calculations show that even a moderate-sized plant would need enormous storage space.This alone would seem to rule out the use of wheat straw, corn stover, and even hay for large-scale ethanol production. For crop residue there is also the problem of soil depletion and erosion when large parts of the stover are removed shortly after harvest. On these grounds, ethyl alcohol from crop residue or other dried crop materials appears unlikely.

A VECTOR, NOT A SOURCE

When ethyl alcohol from biomass has high energy costs, one may question whether this kind of road fuel is really a source of energy or only a way to transform other sources into the desired form, liquid motor fuel for road vehicles.

The question is especially important regarding corn, politically the most attractive of the ethyl alcohol materials but also the most energy intensive. Estimates of the energy costs of crop production vary. Those referred to above (Chambers et al. 1979) are representative of the literature, but the numbers used there are not the only ones. Other analyses show the average energy cost of growing corn to be somewhat lower. But this does not necessarily invalidate the higher estimates. For an activity that is additional to preexisting normal concerns, the relevant cost figures are those at the margins, and they are usually higher than the average ones.

The argument has been made that using energy goods to produce energy goods is rational so long as the output good is more convenient than the input basket of energy goods. The easy analogy is the production of electricity by burning coal. The electricity has much smaller energy content (enthalpy) than the coal burned, but electricity is much more convenient and can be used for many tasks where coal burning would be unpractical.

The analogy is not striking in the case of ethyl alcohol from biomass, especially grains. The input energy in grain production, for instance, is to a large extent already high-grade energy goods such as natural gas, petroleum fuels, and electricity. Thus the gain of transforming some energy goods into a new one may be very partial. The point is highlighted when grain exports are compared with petroleum imports (Dovring 1980).

Nor does it help that other feedstocks have lower energy costs of production than corn. All biomass has some energy cost in harvesting and transportation. At length they all have some fertilizer cost. The latter extends to crop residues, which also contain plant nutrients that must be replaced if they are removed to a distant processing plant. All fertilizer materials have high energy costs. The highest energy costs are those of nitrogen fertilizers, the residue of which is at best retrieved as stockfeed, but often it is destroyed beyond retrieval.

This consideration leads to the question of what other virtues ethyl alcohol may possess besides its energy content.

HIGHER OCTANE, LOWER POLLUTION

The hidden asset of gasohol is in the higher octane rating of alcohol fuels, which contribute to raise the octane rating of the blend with gasoline.

The principal method of raising octane ratings of gasoline used to be adding lead. This practice is being eliminated because of toxic effects, which are especially important in high-density urban areas. Raising the octane level of gasoline without adding lead originally meant some further steps in the refining process, and these added steps also have costs in terms of energy spent in the refinery. Even without those costs, gasoline is the most energy intensive of the petroleum derivatives leaving the refinery.

By contributing to higher octane ratings, gasohol can claim an added energy credit. By saving on energy in the refinery, it contributes to lower total energy costs of road fuel. When this is offset against the energy cost of growing the feedstocks used for ethanol production, the energy cost of alcohol becomes substantially lower. In this way, ethyl alcohol, even from corn, may contribute to a better energy balance, the equivalent of contributing some additional energy rather than being a mere vector. The question posed in straight energy analysis would seem answered in favor of gasohol.

Subsequent research and development has focused on still other means of raising the octane rating of gasoline by a variety of chemical additives, whose production in many cases is less energy intensive than alcohol production. They may require even less than the energy expense remaining to be charged to the ethanol when the octane credit has been subtracted. If some of these substances are successful, alcohol as an octane booster may become obsolete.

Another merit of alcohol fuels is that they contribute less to air pollution than do the petroleum-derived fuels. Both ethanol and methanol have simpler molecules than gasoline or diesel fuel. They burn more completely and leave less residue. In this regard, methanol is generally rated as superior to ethanol. In any event, the pollution abatement of the alcohol element in gasoline is minor compared to that of the neat alcohol fuels, and for such purpose ethanol is not a serious alternative.

A MERE BYPRODUCT?

The question of distributing costs between joint products sometimes leads to the conclusion that ethanol from grain is not a main product but a byproduct. The main product would then be the DDG or DDGS. The value of this high-grade livestock feed could be so large a part of the cost of corn as feedstock (and of the processing cost) that the alcohol could be regarded as a minor product. This would be particularly likely in firms where "corn refining" means recovering all products, including the heavy alcohols and the carbon dioxide that small distilleries are unable to capture.

If alcohol is a byproduct, why does fuel ethanol need tax relief in order to be profitable? If DDG(S) is a main product, its price ought to cover enough of the costs to allow the alcohol to be sold for what the market can bear. The tax subsidy may have been thought of mainly as a help to small distilleries. In practice it is captured by all producers. Ironically it even accrued (for a time, at least) to ethanol imported from Brazil.

The question of main product versus byproduct is far from simple. In large corn refineries, alcohol alternates with corn sweeteners, depending on market demand and price as these vary from time to time. The byproduct argument becomes stronger in times of low fuel prices, but, whenever the price of gasoline is high, alcohol comes closer to being the main product. The relative advantage of large and small distilleries also changes with changing relative prices.

The relative prominence of each of the joint products can change for the converse reasons, too. High-protein feed may be thought of as a main product so long as its price is high. Unlike alcohol, which would vary in price only with the price of gasoline, the price of protein feed in DDG(S) would vary with that of competing products such as soybean meal or whole corn and with the volume of its own supply. So far, DDG(S) has been a minor component in the market for livestock feed. If the fuel ethanol activity were to grow to much larger proportions, the supply of DDG(S) would also become much larger, eventually large enough to depress its own price. In that case, the question of byproduct versus main product would become different. It is to be assumed that a much larger volume of fuel ethanol would reflect high gasoline prices as its "push"; hence, the falling feed prices would be matched by rising fuel prices.

The question of joint products would become different in an integrated farm-level system intended for local energy supply.

ETHANOL FOR FARMS

The main thrust of this book is to show that methanol is the most likely alternative for processing biomass into liquid fuel. Ethanol, as an element in gasohol blends, appears to be a blind alley, a route that will not lead us very far. However, it is possible that ethanol could serve in one limited sector, namely agriculture. Alcohol distilleries on farms could serve as a way of securing local fuel supply directly to farms without relying very much on distant supply sources. The reason for this possible exception is that farms, as widely scattered customers, could in this way become less dependent on other sectors. They could also reap certain special advantages that would follow from the farm-level, decentralized operation of such distilleries and related installations.

There could be two main variants of farm-level ethanol distilleries. They could be distilleries using grain (usually corn) in the conventional way, producing stillage (wet distillers' grain) for immediate use on nearby farms. Or, using different feedstocks, farm-level distilleries could produce lower-grade stillage to be used not as livestock feed but as feedstock for gaseous fuels.

The former would resemble what has so far been the main model of an ethanol distillery. Corn (or other crop material) would be ground or crushed, placed into a tank for enzyme treatment to turn it into sugar, which then would be fermented into hydrous alcohol (beer) to be distilled into hydrous alcohol for use in farm machines. The fermentation residue would not have to be dried into DDG(S) but could be fed to livestock on nearby farms according to standing contracts, thus avoiding any prolonged storage and any deterioration in storage.

This type of distillery would have several advantages over the commercial ones. The price of the feedstock would be farm-gate price, not wholesale price as in the case of the large and the medium-sized distilleries. This is a saving on the marketing margin. The cost of distilling the hydrous alcohol would be lower because 10 percent water can be tolerated (or even be of advantage) when the alcohol is used as neat fuel, with no gasoline blended in. The value of the fuel to the user would be at retail cost; thus, the marketing margin is saved here,too. Finally the stillage would not have to be dried, which is a saving on energy and operation. And the value of the stillage to the users would be at retail, one more saving on the marketing margin. It is assumed that the distillery is owned by and operated by or for a consortium of nearby farmers.

Under conditions as they exist in the central Corn Belt, such a system could supply all the fuel for field operations while using about 5 percent of the cropland. This is low-cost traction power; in horse farming, for example in Europe, it was calculated that horses ate what grew on 10 percent of the crop- and pasture-land; the cost of traction power was 10 percent of the land.

The other system would be even more integrated with farm operations, but it would not necessarily produce any livestock feed. It would be better adapted for areas where livestock is of secondary importance as in east-central Illinois and northwestern Iowa. In the future, if animal husbandry declines as it well may in response to gradually better high-protein foods from crops, the system could apply to much larger areas.

In this system, the fuel feedstock need not be grain; it might to good advantage be green silage. The material could still be row crops such as corn for silage, but more likely it would be tall grasses, alfalfa, or still other field feed crops such as Jerusalem artichoke (*Helianthus tuberosus*, Kansas sunflower) that can be maintained as permanent vegetation with no tillage or, at most, tillage at long intervals. If silage crops are harvested at the right stage, they are full of starch with little or no cellulose. In silage tanks they can be kept for long times, with at most 5 percent deterioration during long-term storage. As with grain, the ground or mashed silage would be enzyme treated into sugar, to be fermented as in corn alcohol. Again, the alcohol need only be distilled to 90 percent (180 proof) when it is intended for use on nearby farms, as neat fuel, and the bookkeeping could show the same advantages as in corn alcohol in saving on marketing margins.

The stillage, however, would not be as valuable as when it is the residue of corn. It could then instead be placed in an anaerobic digester to produce methane, to be used as gaseous fuel. In the first place this would supply the operational fuel for the distillery itself, which thus would be one more degree insulated from the larger fuel markets. It is likely that eventually the methane could be sufficient also for other energy needs on the farms including household use. This could be facilitated if the stillage were blended with other materials such as crop residue (to the extent such can safely be removed from the fields).

Such a fuel system for farms would keep farming areas less vulnerable to any future supply interruptions, for whatever cause such might occur. As a farm-level industry such distilleries would also supply additional employment especially in the off seasons of agriculture. Concentrating on silage crops would remove the objections against using more land for row crops as would happen if corn is the feedstock; to the contrary, the fuel-producing land would be plowed only at long intervals if at all. Erosion stress on the land might thus be reduced. The pressure of excess production on the farm would also be somewhat reduced because the farmers no longer would need to produce that part of their salable crops needed to buy fuel.

This kind of energy system could eventually cover large parts of the farm industry. Nationwide, it would represent only a minor part of the solution to the problem of liquid fuels for the future, for the whole energy demand of agriculture in the United States is only on the magnitude of 3 percent to 4 percent of the national energy budget.

NO ANSWER TO THE NEXT OIL CRUNCH

Ethyl alcohol, by way of gasohol blends, could never be a major part of the solution to the problem of liquid motor fuel. As grain alcohol, the merit of having valuable joint products (however these may be classified, as byproducts or as main output) does not help when the central fact is that the yield of liquid fuel is as low as 250 gallons an acre and is obtained at high cost of energy input. The initiative toward gasohol was supply driven; it never reflected a realistic assessment of future demand.

Even the target of 10 percent alcohol to be blended with all gasoline appears unreachable when the alcohol has to be ethanol. But even if this target were reached, this supply would keep us going only as long as any short-fall of transportation fuel did not seriously exceed 10 percent. All indications are that the need for other road fuels will be much larger than that within about a decade.

It is logical then to warn that the gasohol route is a blind alley and that other avenues must be sought that can lead to a secure and independent energy future for the United States. The methanol alternative will have to be explored both as to its possible scope (Chapters 5, 6, and 7), its cost of production beyond the feedstock costs (Chapter 8), and its technical use in road motors (Chapter 9). From those premises we will summarize what appears to be a feasible future energy scenario (Chapter 10).

5

BIOMASS PRODUCTION AS LAND-USE DIVERSIFICATION

One of the large problems that biomass energy production will answer is the long-standing need for diversification in the use of agricultural land in the United States. The issue cannot be held apart entirely from the need for soil conservation, which in part has been used to intercept some of the most pressing land surplus. In this chapter we will concentrate on the economic need and the possibilities for land-use diversification. The next chapter will deal with the conservation issue as a parallel, but not an additional, argument about future land use.

Several approaches are possible if we want to determine how much land is surplus in U.S. agriculture. Traditionally, estimates have focused on conditions as they are, assuming this country would continue its inherited eating habits and its current or recent role as exporter of farm goods. Such an assumption of continuing "as is" is, of course, the simplest assumption one can make; it requires less explanation than is necessary if we also assume that things will change, as they certainly must in many ways.

Continuing dietary habits specifically assumes continuing large consumption of animal products, despite the changes that have taken place and are taking place. Since 1940, margarine has to a large extent displaced butter with considerable land saving as a result. In recent years there have been changes in meat consumption, tending toward more poultry and less red meat. Poultry production also requires less land and less energy than producing red meat. Among the sweeteners, those derived from corn are now produced in larger volume than is traditional sugar from both beets and cane, both home grown and imported. New types of foods based entirely or mainly on crops come from the food chemistry laboratories and slowly work their way into U.S. diets. Assuming constant eating habits is therefore not very realistic. Current policy has generally tended to inhibit changes in the composition of the food basket. Under a different set of policies, such changes might be accelerated.

HOW MUCH CROPLAND?

For the large land-use categories, we must admit some inaccuracy in the statistics and some wavering in the definitions. In recent years the Census of Agriculture has tended to give figures that are too low; sometimes it gives figures too high because of double counting. Even the overall figures for the areas of whole states are not above criticism (Dovring 1983).

Even on their own terms, the statistics are not entirely unambiguous. For agricultural land use, we are given figures for cropland that include summer fallow in the year when this particular acreage carried no crops, because the fallow was part of the acreage that produced those crops over the years. Cropland used for crops also includes lands on which the crops failed in the census year. Cropland used for crops further includes cropland diverted from production because of federal acreage reduction programs. There is also something called cropland pasture. Across all these categories is the "conservation reserve," most of which is used in one way or another. Only a minor part is actually enrolled for conservation programs. Most of the following data come from *Agricultural Resources* 1986. Some are illustrated in Figure 5.1.

The long and short of all this is that the United States has about 470 million acres (190 million hectares) of cropland. In recent years the use of this land for crops (including crop failure and summer fallow) has varied from 387 million acres (1981) to 333 million (1983). The low figure in 1983 was due to the federal program of Payment In Kind (PIK), which gave farmers stored crops (mainly grains) on condition that they idled as much land as would have been needed to produce those in-kind crop payments. This program reduced the carryover stocks in government ownership, and it idled 78 million acres, which ordinarily would have been used for crops and pasture. In 1987, land used for crops totaled 330 million acres. Some of the variations are shown in Table 5.1.

Comparing those figures with the total cropland area of 470 million acres, we conclude that acreages varying from 87 million to 140 million acres have not been used for crops in recent years. This is only partly because of federal programs. Much cropland is more or less permanently left idle and is designated as cropland pasture.

Cropland pasture has varied from 88 million acres in 1969 to 65 million

Figure 5.1
U.S. Land Base in 1977 (Million acres)

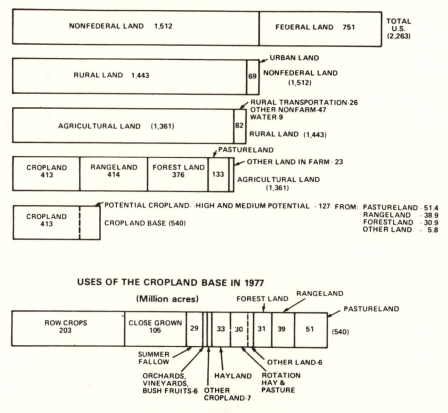

Source: National Agricultural Lands Study (NALS), USDA, Washington, D.C., 1981

in 1982. The figure for cropland pasture is given only in the years when a Census of Agriculture is taken. The most recent one was in 1982. We expect a Census of Agriculture to be taken in 1987, but it will not be published for some time. For the years when there is no Census of Agriculture, we may estimate the area of cropland pasture by subtraction. Thus, in 1986 use for crops was 357 million acres, diverted acres (set-aside) 49 million, and enrolled in conservation reserve 9 million. That is 413 million acres, leaving about 55 million, which we may assume would be called cropland pasture.

Much of the acreage used for pasture is actually rotated, so that in each year some part of the cropland used for crops is land that in other years is called cropland pasture. This might be called a long-fallow system. Land that is rotated in this manner is a larger area than the area of cropland pasture in any one year.

Table 5.1
Major Uses of Cropland, United States[1]

Cropland	1969	1978	1982	1983	1984	1985	1986	1987[2]
	M i l l i o n a c r e s							
Cropland used for crops	333	369	383	333	373	372	357	330
Cropland harvested	286	330	347	294	337	334	316	292
Cropland failure	6	7	5	5	6	7	9	6
Cultivated summer fallow	41	32	31	34	30	31	32	32
Idle cropland[3]	51	26	21	..	..	..	..	..
Cropland pasture[3]	88	76	65	..	..	..	..	..
Total cropland[3]	472	471	469	..	..	..	..	..

" = Data not available
[1] Includes the conterminous 48 states
[2] Preliminary figures
[3] Estimated only for years in which a Census of Agriculture was not taken

Source: *Agricultural Resources*, USDA, September 1987, Table 1.

On the one hand, some of the cropland used for pasture is, however, of dubious value as cropland and seldom, if ever, used in that way. On the other hand, some of the lands designated in the statistics as permanent pasture are good enough so that they might be converted to cropland use if this were to the advantage of the owners or operators. The total estimate of 470 million acres of cropland in the United States is therefore as good a minimum figure as any we are likely to find. Other estimates place total potential cropland higher.

Of the entire cropland base, one-half is located in the Corn Belt and northern plains states, a total of nine states. If we add the three lake states, then the twelve states of the Midwest have 58 percent to 59 percent of the country's cropland.

Farmers have much other land besides cropland. Of the total estimated 2,265 million acres of the United States, more than half, or 1200 million acres, is enumerated as being in farms. Farms have nearly all the cropland. They have pasturelands totaling somewhat more acres than the cropland, and this is the bulk, but not yet all, of the pasture land in the country, some of which is public domain. Farms have woodlands of about 200 million acres, less than one-third of all the woodlands in the United States. What the production potentials may be of these lands depends on a multitude of geographic features including topography and climate, above all rainfall.

CROPLAND REQUIREMENTS IN RECENT DEBATE

Despite all the worry about surplus agricultural production, there have been repeated inquiries whether the United States in the future will have enough agricultural land to provide food and fiber for its people.

The first of these inquiries in the postwar period was the USDA *A 50-Year Look Ahead at U.S. Agriculture* (1959). For the year 2010, alternative population projections foresaw 300, 370, or 440 million people. Crop yields were projected to increase at rather moderate rates. Alternatively, exports of agricultural products were assumed to remain at the level of 1957 or to increase by 52 percent.

The high population projection combined with high exports led to the conclusion that 230 million acres of new cropland would have to be found. This figure represents the utmost amount that could be mobilized from underutilized land resources. It was assumed that urban expansion and other nonagricultural land uses would absorb 33 million acres. Apparently, a cropland base of 665 million acres was thought possible. With 370 million people there would be a need for 122 million acres of new cropland, of which 25 million acres would be absorbed by other uses, leaving a net increase of 97 million acres. With a population of 300 million, no new cropland would be needed. In each case, the export alternatives would mean a difference of about 45 million acres.

Using subsequent statistics we find that the population trend now points to a likely population figure of 300 million in 2010. Actual population was 227 million in 1980 and 242 million in 1986, indicating a rate of increase of just under 1 percent a year.

Recent statistics indicate a larger and larger surplus of cropland, despite exports having expanded more than expected. From 1960 to 1980, U.S. grain exports rose more than fourfold—from 25 million tons to 112 million. The reason this increase in external demand did not cause any land shortage in the United States is that the increases in crop yields far surpassed what had been expected. Several crops had considerably higher yields in the mid-1980s than the cited study had projected for 2010. Others had higher yields in the 1980s than would be expected from the rates of increase assumed for the whole period.

There have been several other studies of farmland base since 1959. One of the most recent is the USDA *National Agricultural Lands Study* (1981), or NALS. It was done in response to concerns about future shortage of land for agricultural production. There had been vigorous expansion of nonagricultural land uses; the 1960s and 1970s saw a great deal of urban decentralization when people moved from the inner cities to suburban and exurban settlements. Despite this, the NALS did not envision any immediate likelihood of land shortage in the United States. The cropland base is shown as 540 million acres; 413 million acres are actually in cropland use, with a medium potential of 127 million of which 51 million could be reclaimed from pastureland, 39 million from rangeland, 31 million from forestland, and 6 million from other land.

Implicitly, the problem is not shortage, but excess supply. Research in the 1970s and 1980s deals more with possibilities of retiring land from crop production and of increasing the protection of erodible farmlands than with increasing output.

USES OF CROPLAND IN RECENT TIME

Most of the cropland in the United States is used to produce food or feed. Cereal grains have occupied 180 million acres recently, with corn in the first place, about 70 to 75 million acres, wheat second, 60 to 65 million; sorghum, barley, oats, and rice in minor positions; and rye on rather small acreage. Other prominent crops are soybeans and hay, each with more than 60 million acres in most years. Oilseeds other than soybeans cover much smaller acreages, as do sugar crops, peanuts, and potatoes. Fruits and vegetables between themselves occupy only about 6 million acres. Of the nonfood crops, cotton alone is on the magnitude of 10 million acres; tobacco occupies less than 1 million acres.

These proportions have been quite different in the past. Both cotton and potatoes once occupied several times the acreages they do now. Rising yields have offset declining acreages as markets did not expand apace. Corn has declined somewhat in acreage even as yield quadrupled over a few decades, leaving a much larger marketable output. The large newcomer is the soybean, which was only a minor crop about 1930.

The increase in production possibilities is highlighted by the expansion of irrigated acreage, which rose from about 30 million acres in the 1950s to 50 million in the late 1970s. Recently there has been some decline in irrigated acreage, to 45 million, in response to rising energy prices that strongly affect irrigation pumping. Irrigation has been and is to a large extent favored by federal subsidies, which thus help increase production even as other federal programs try to curb surplus production.

Discussing current use of U.S. farmland, we first look at the portion of the land that produces crops for export. Next we consider withdrawal of land from crop production for surplus control, mainly by federal programs, and for erosion control. Finally we have to question how much cropland will at length be needed to feed the nation.

LAND USE FOR EXPORT CROPS

Few farms grow crops specifically for exports; they usually grow them for the market in general, which thereafter proceeds to allocate the crops it purchases between domestic use and exports, some of them indirectly through processed products. Data on acreage used for export crops are therefore derived statistics reflecting certain averages rather than direct observation of export-oriented production.

Exports claimed the output of 60 to 65 million acres a year about 1960. The share of exports then rose to over 100 million acres in the 1970s, and to about 125 million acres 1979–1983. The following two years acreage for exports again fell below 100 million acres. This was not because of production being intended for fewer exports but because exports fell as a consequence of the high exchange rates for the dollar. Under better export prospects, the share would have remained about 125 million acres.

Thus the export share in acreage rose more than under the expansion alternative in the 1959 USDA *50-Year Look Ahead,* which expected to add at most 45 million acres to export acreage by 2010. The same derived data allows us to conclude that cropland acreage actually used to produce for the domestic U.S. market fell from 260 million acres about 1960 to about 225 million in the late 1970s and early 1980s. Per capita cropland used for domestic consumption fell from 1.5 acres about 1960 to barely 1 acre recently. Production has increased at a faster rate than domestic demand; export demand has not quite taken up the difference, and hence the United States has a problem of excess agricultural output reflecting a land base that is larger than needed in the near term and in all likelihood in the long run too.

One of the standard prescriptions for improving the economic position of U.S. farmers is to make them more productive so that they will be able to compete more successfully on international markets. This, however, risks increasing even more the amounts of products that U.S. farmers must export in order to balance their books. This strategy can be questioned on several grounds. U.S. exports already include half of all cereal grains that move in international trade, nearly the same proportion in wheat, a much larger one in corn, and an overwhelming majority of all soybeans traded internationally. There are serious competitors such as Canada, Australia, Argentina, and Brazil (for soybeans). For each of these countries, farm exports actually are even more vital than they are for the United States.

An opposite strategy for the United States would be to retrench, plan less export production as a means to better sustain the international prices. To some extent this is done now with the federal acreage limitation programs. To do even more of the same would be very cumbersome for the federal treasury. Instead, one would wish there were some alternative use for the land that now produces so much for export that the sheer volume of it tends to depress U.S. farm prices.

The question of future export strategy can be examined from several viewpoints. One is the cost of export crops at the margin in comparison with export prices. Another one is in the balance of energy used to grow the crops (or the energy that could be obtained by processing the crops for energy in comparison with the energy obtained from imported oil) and the relative prices of grain exports and oil imports. A final view questions how much U.S. agricultural exports are needed in order to feed the hungry in the world and how far this facet of the international economy helps or hinders the development of the entire world community.

MARGINAL COST OF EXPORT CROPS

U.S. agricultural exports consist mainly of seven major crops: wheat, rice, corn, sorghum, soybeans, cotton, and tobacco. Each of these crops exceeded 1 percent of annual value of agricultural exports in recent years, and no other crop that can be identified singly meets this criterion. Together, the seven crops approach three-fourths of all U.S. export value of agricultural products, and they equal more than four-fifths of all export crop value. Tobacco occupies only a rather small acreage and so can be left out of our discussion. The other six crops together occupy about 230 million acres of cropland, about half of which produces for export.

Export crops other than those just mentioned cover only minor portions of all U.S. agricultural exports. They include a large number of items, and many of them are matched by imports of the same or some similar product. The same is true of exports of animal products, which are nearly balanced by imports in the same general category. The seven major crops, by contrast, are represented on the import side by only very small amounts. Thus these seven crops are truly the mainstay of the country's agricultural export trade.

Disregarding tobacco, the cost of producing the other six crops was investigated by means of a data series called *Firm Enterprise Data System*. It was published by the USDA for production regions within the states for several years up to 1981 and for whole states only for 1982 and 1983 (Dovring 1985, 1987a, 1987b). Data were analyzed for 1981–1983 and 1978.

The results are consistent in showing two things. One is that in nearly all budget areas, the rate of return to costs (other than land costs) were lower in 1981–1982 than in 1978. The other is that the rate of return to nonland resources is very different according to production areas, leaving many areas in a marginal or even submarginal position in one crop or another or in all of them.

One consistent feature is that nearly all irrigation budgets show low or negative returns to resources in 1981–1983 and usually lower than average returns in 1978 also. Negative returns are particularly striking in the southern plains region (Texas, Oklahoma, New Mexico, and eastern Colorado) and extending into western Kansas. The suggestion that irrigation should be abandoned or greatly reduced in such irrigation areas would lead to some reduction in exportable crop quantitites as well as some improvement in the rate of return to exportable crops. The difference that this would make, however, is minor. Much larger differences could be obtained by also withdrawing from growing these export crops in regions where the rate of return to nonland resources is low—in any event far below the average for the crop in general. Such would be the case for corn in Texas, North Carolina, Georgia, and other southeastern states.

In wheat production, rates of return were generally low in hard wheats in North Dakota and Oklahoma, and in soft red winter wheat in all the southeastern states including Tennessee and Kentucky. Grain sorghum showed low rates of return in the irrigation budgets of New Mexico, California, Texas, Oklahoma, and Colorado as well as in dryland budgets in Texas and Colorado. For rice, the budgets from southwestern Louisiana and the Texas Gulf Coast had very low rates of return in 1981–1983 but much higher ones in 1978. An ongoing upward trend in rice yields may remedy the situation for all the southcentral rice areas. California's Sacramento Valley appears in a category apart, with about equally high rates of return in 1981–1983 and in 1978.

In soybeans, rates of return differ somewhat less between areas than in the cereal grain crops, but here too it is evident that all the budgets in the southeastern states are well below average—lowest in Alabama and South Carolina. Irrigated soybeans in Nebraska also show lower rates of return than average. Cotton also displayed low rates of return to nonland resources in the southeastern states as well as in irrigation budgets in Oklahoma, Arizona, and Texas.

The results cannot be read to mean that all production of the crops thus analyzed should be abandoned in the states mentioned or that there should be no reductions in other states. Quite to the contrary, we must assume that there is variation also within states and budget areas; therefore, some of these crops may remain viable in parts of the states and areas of low rates of return. We must assume also that some subareas or individual farms in other states would have been found marginal or submarginal if the data had allowed detailed analysis.

Eliminating production of export crops in areas where they are grown with low rates of return to nonland inputs would do several things. It would reduce the average cost of production for each crop, increase the rate of return per unit of output actually produced, and reduce the exportable quantities of each crop. This would remove some of the downward pressure on the prices of each crop.

A strategic plan for withdrawing land from production of export crops in the geographic areas where the costs are highest would thus lead to less export agriculture, but the remaining export agriculture would be more profitable, both to the farmers producing those crops and to the country as a whole.

The counterpart of this proposal is that to set such a solution in motion, alternative use must be found for the land no longer used for export crops. Unlike the federal set-aside programs of recent years, which remove from production some fraction of each farmer's land whether it is good, average, or marginal, the proposal set forth here would focus on the marginal lands, leaving the good and the average lands intact to produce without setting anything aside. This in itself would lower cost of production and raise the rates of return to resources used for those crops, including returns to land, and it would make possible higher rates of remuneration to labor and management.

TO EXPORT OR TO BURN?

The next approach to the problem of surplus or low-remunerative crop exports is to ask what advantage the country as a whole has in continuing crop exports. Such exports are a large portion of our export trade, and they are needed, so we are often told, in order to pay for necessary imports such as petroleum. In the late 1970s when petroleum prices were high, agricultural exports at rather high prices covered about two-thirds of the bill for oil imports. In some recent years, with prices much lower on both oil and crops, proceeds from agricultural exports have just about matched the oil imports.

Merely comparing dollar amounts, however, is not sufficient. Oil is an energy good, and crops are energy intensive goods, which offer us the option of converting them into energy goods. How this trades off depends upon the proportions between the energy quantities as well as the prices at which they are traded. The analysis is by no means simple, but some indications can be given (Dovring 1980).

The energy used to produce crops consists for the most part of high-grade fuels such as gasoline, diesel fuel, and natural gas, with some input of electricity. To pursue the analysis, it has been necessary to include also the energy used indirectly, both by the industries making and delivering energy goods and by those making other inputs for agricultural production (Dovring 1984a).

For example, it was found that in the Midwest a bushel of corn, on the average, costs 100 thousand Btu of energy. Comparing this with crude oil, which holds about 5.8 million Btu per barrel of 42 gallons, it seems that a barrel could cost the equivalent of 58 bushels of corn before the energy input into corn production would begin to exceed the energy value purchased at this high price.

This is, however, modified in two ways. The energy cost of corn is nearly all high-grade fuel, but a barrel of crude oil is not. Refineries will leave off some low-grade products, even in the United States, and they consume the equivalent of 15 percent to 20 percent of their own enthalpy as process heat in the refinery. The tolerable cost of oil in terms of energy used to grow corn is a good deal less than 58 bushels. Another complication comes from variation in the energy cost of growing corn. Analysis of production budgets in the Midwest shows that some of these use almost 150 thousand Btu a bushel already on dry land and up to 200 thousand on some irrigated areas. This would bring down the corn/energy cost of a barrel of oil to 37 or 29 bushels of corn. In reality the cost is less because of the difference between crude oil and refined fuels.

The prices to consider are not those in international grain trade, which must pay for storage, brokerage, and transportation (itself an energy-using activity), but the farm prices, which at present are less than $2 a bushel for corn. If the price of oil rises to $40 as it did not long ago, it would take 20 bushels (or more) of corn to buy a barrel at that price. That price could come close to breaking even, for irrigated corn at least. Thus grain exports are not always and under all circumstances a profitable way to buy petroleum in international markets.

If we consider the alternative of converting the grain into ethanol, we get a different trade-off. Each bushel could yield 2.5 gallons of alcohol, which, in its function as an octane booster, must be considered of equal fuel value with the gasoline. Retaining the corn and making ethanol from it, we would save about 6 percent of a barrel of oil (or more, considering the lower equivalent of crude oil) and retain DDG and other valuable byproducts. Selling the corn in international markets we part with all its contents; there are no byproducts to retain.

A gallon of gasoline contains 125 thousand Btu. Thus the alcohol from corn (as an octane booster) becomes the equivalent of 313 thousand Btu, and it would take only 18.5 bushels of corn to produce the equivalent of the energy in a barrel of crude oil. Again crude oil is not quite equivalent, so we would need something less than 18.5 bushels to redeem the same energy. We have not begun to put a price on the DDG or other byproducts that should at least (and probably more than) pay for the cost of processing the corn into alcohol. At 18.5 bushels, and $40 a barrel for crude oil, corn would need to be at least $2.16 at farm gate, which is higher than the current price.

Such calculations can be refined. The purpose here is to show that the advantage of importing oil and exporting grain to pay for it is by no means self-evident at all levels of prices of the two commodities, corn and crude oil. And again, we have not factored in the military and political costs of securing the supply of crude oil for import from distant supply sources.

A simpler and more straightforward comparison can be made in the case of methanol from biomass. On good land, an acre can produce gross fuel well in excess of 1,000 gallons an acre (Herendeen and Dovring 1984). Net fuel may well be about 1,000 gallons. A gallon of methanol contains 65 thousand Btu, but the propulsion value is 20 percent higher, so the gallon of methanol will replace 78 thousand Btu of gasoline or diesel. Thus an acre in high-yielding biomass for methanol production would deliver some 78 million Btu equivalent of propulsion power.

If instead the same acre produces 100 bushels of corn for export, it will buy 12.5 barrels of oil at $16 a barrel, which brings us 72.5 million Btu of crude oil and a somewhat smaller amount of refinery fuel equivalent. At $40 a barrel, the 100 bushels at $2 a bushel would buy only 5 barrels of oil, or 29 million Btu of crude oil, again a somewhat smaller amount of refinery fuel equivalent. In terms of methanol, in a future with high and insecure prices of crude oil it is easy to see that we will do much better growing fuel feedstock than exporting grain.

EXPORT TO FEED THE WORLD?

U.S. export agriculture is often discussed as a service to the world. Our crops in storage make it unnecessary for other countries to spend resources on carryover stocks, and U.S. grain is always available for stopgap famine relief.

Crop exports from the United States come in three broad categories. First there are emergency shipments to countries or areas stricken with acute famine. Second there is foreign economic aid in the form of shipments of surplus agricultural commodities. Finally, and most important, U.S. agricultural exports contribute to feeding the world, at costs which might well be higher without this contribution to international trade.

At a close look, the beneficial nature of our crop exports is less evident than it might seem at a bird's-eye view. Famine relief is, in any event, a small part of these shipments. The main difficulty about famine relief is not in the quantities required. The rich countries of the world could always supply these quantities. The main difficulty is instead in the logistics of moving the supplies to their destination. Countries so poor they incur famine in our time are poorly equipped with transportation facilities and other infrastructure needed to deliver the emergency supplies.

Foreign economic aid in the form of shipments of U.S. surplus agricultural products is another matter. Such shipments total much greater quantities than famine relief shipments, yet they remain a minor portion of all U.S. agricultural exports. The history of such aid, since the concept was started in the 1950s, is long and complicated. The basic flaw is in the very concept of aid as surplus disposal, rather than aid because it was what was needed. In an extreme case, powdered or condensed milk shipped to countries where milk was not a part of the habitual diet caused severe discomfort. In such cases, a lesson is soon learned. More serious is the dislocation that gratuitous or very low-cost food shipments could cause a recipient country's economy by depriving that country's farmers of some part of their market. Secondarily, such aid shipments also could reduce the normal market outlets for other agricultural export countries.

The remedy against dislocation in the recipient country's agricultural economy was soon formulated. Mordecai Ezekiel, U.S. economist working for the F.A.O. of the United Nations, explained on the basis of econometric calculations that food aid would be beneficial on condition that it is combined with other economic aid, in cash or in goods but in such proportions that the whole aid package becomes a net addition to the whole of the recipient country's economy (FAO 1956). In other words, the food aid must not exceed the proportions that additional food imports would have if all the aid were extended in the form of cash or cash equivalent. When food aid seriously exceeds those proportions—and they depend on income level and other circumstances within the country—then it is likely to cause dislocations resulting in retarded agricultural development within the recipient country. Such a result is the opposite of what economic development aid should be.

The advice was sound, but it was far from always followed. Food aid is supply driven, but economic aid in general is not. On the whole, the United States, as well as most other high-income countries, has held foreign economic aid to very modest proportions. The insight that such aid can also serve as promotion of future exports—and not only of farm goods—was seldom brought to bear on foreign economic aid. On balance, therefore, foreign-aid shipments of surplus agricultural products from the United States have probably done more harm than good. There are many complications in individual cases, and they might draw in one direction or another, but, on the whole, food aid has not been a great success.

This leads us to the bulk of the problem, which is the position of the United States as the largest supplier of agricultural products to international markets. On such markets, we are in competition both with other exporting nations and with the world's farmers, not the least those in importing countries. Often the governments of low- or middle-income countries will import agricultural products as a means of containing food costs for their urban populations because these are the people most likely to riot against a government when food prices rise. Such short-sighted import policies serve to retard agricultural development, much as that would be needed for other reasons.

The world is not in dire need of imports from the United States. Costs of production as conventionally measured are often lower in U.S. agriculture than the costs of additional production in the importing countries. But conventional cost accounting is not all that is needed to understand agricultural protectionism. In the present drive for free trade in agricultural products, many Americans fail to understand that other countries may be acting quite rationally when they protect domestic agriculture. At least, it is often difficult to measure what damage agricultural protection might cause.

Switzerland is an extreme case where very high levels of protection of domestic agriculture has been in harmony with high prosperity and rising levels of per-capita income. Now the European Economic Community is repeating the same experience. No doubt the EEC could obtain its food a little cheaper by producing less of it and importing more of it. But this is so on the surface only. Keeping a high level of agricultural production, the countries of the EEC also make more complete use of their land and their agricultural labor, which is precisely the same advantage that the United States was thought to gain from maintaining surplus production to the extent of increasing its food exports both concessional (as aid) and commercial. Recently, Japan is repeating the experience that Switzerland and the EEC have found to be to their advantage. While importing a good deal of their food supply, the Japanese are even so protecting domestic agriculture at very high levels. In so doing they insure basic food supply at home (a strategic consideration) and maintain some of those traditional national values that many nations cherish.

From international trade statistics we can see also that most of U.S. farm exports go to countries with high or medium income levels, such as EEC countries, Japan, Korea, and the Soviet Union. Latin America, which might well be able to feed itself under somewhat different economic policies, does not rank high among the customers. India and several other Asian nations are now much closer to supplying their own food needs, thanks in no small degree to the U.S. sponsored and financed work on crop improvement known as the "Green Revolution." No doubt there will be more of that, given the incentives for farmers in those countries—incentives that are not necessarily improved by continuing food imports. The weakest part of the low-income world is Africa, which actually receives about one-tenth of the food imports in the world. The bulk of that goes to Egypt and North Africa, with tropical Africa much lower on the ladder, large as the need may be. But even here we may question whether the short-run advantages of food imports are really consistent with the long-run need for agricultural development in Africa. North Africa including Egypt is a special case because of shortage of water.

The recent call for free international trade in agricultural products may therefore prove on a close look to be to the one-sided advantage of the United States, and in the relatively short run at that. The world as a whole will fare better if each nation first takes charge of its essential internal affairs among which food farming is more essential than most other parts of an economy. In the long run, such nation-level protection of agriculture may well prove to do most for an accelerated economic development of the world, to the ultimate benefit also of the United States.

The stark fact is that U.S. agricultural science, combined with very competent farm management, has created within this country a farm plant that is far too large for the country's own needs, at the same time that the projection of advanced (and often U.S. invented or sponsored) agricultural progress elsewhere causes the world to have less and less use for a share in our farm bounty.

So far, the reaction to this problem within the United States has been uncertain and faltering. In July 1987, a spokesman for the USDA hoped for better export prospects in the years ahead, and a figure was mentioned for coarse grain exports by 1990 that was no greater than the figure about 1980. Along with such hopes, the time worn but patently insufficient expedient of land withdrawal is continued in a way that should reveal the nature of the problem.

NONUSE OF LAND FOR SURPLUS CONTROL

Removing farmland from production has been practiced since the 1950s. It was one of the responses to the surplus production problems, along with the beginning of the food aid program under Public Law 480. The Soil Bank began in 1955, and signups continued until 1960 when the total was between 25 and 30 million acres, usually on ten-year contracts for no agricultural use. Along with it, a short-term Acreage Reserve Program also withheld land on shorter contracts. This program culminated in 1957 with 21 million acres, at a cost of over $600 million in that year.

Beginning in 1961, cropland was withheld from specific crops under a variety of arrangements, reaching peaks of 43 million acres in 1966 and over 50 million acres in 1969 and 1970, at which time most of the Soil Bank contracts had expired. Beginning in 1973, these acreage nonuse programs were discontinued, and there were none for cereal grain crops from 1974 to 1977. In 1978, the year of the first alcohol fuel

Table 5.2
Base Acreage Diverted from Production under Federal Farm Programs,
United States

Crop	1969	1978	1982	1983	1984	1985	1986	1987
		M i l l i o n a c r e s						
Corn	27.2	6.1	2.1	32.2	3.9	5.4	13.9	21.1
Grain sorghum	7.5	1.4	0.7	5.7	0.6	0.9	2.4	3.9
Barley	4.4	0.8	0.4	1.1	0.5	0.7	1.8	2.9
Oats			0.1	0.3	0.1	0.1	0.4	0.9
Wheat	11.1	9.6	5.8	30.0	18.6	18.8	20.9	19.3
Cotton		0.3	1.6	6.8	2.5	3.6	3.4	3.3
Rice			0.4	1.8	0.8	1.2	1.3	1.3
Long-term diversion	7.8						2.0	15.8[1]
Total[2]	58.0	18.3	11.1	78.0	26.9	30.7	49.0	68.5

[1] Cropland idled for 10 years in the Conservation Reserve Program. Another 7 million acres have been enrolled in the 1988 program.
[2] Because of rounding, crop acreages may not sum to totals.

Source: Agricultural Resources, USDA, September 1987, Table 5.

inquiries in the DOE, some 24 million acres were signed up for withholding from crop production. This should have reduced potential grain output by some 36 million tons. This was as yet much less than in some past years, for example, 1969/70 and 1972/73, when some 75 to 80 million tons of grain production were foregone by acreage set-aside programs.

The 1980s have seen steady increase in acreage set-aside programs. From 11 million acres in 1982, the total climbed to 49 million acres in 1986. Most of this was land that would have produced wheat or corn. There was also some diversion from cotton, but none from soybeans. Some data are shown in Table 5.2.

As if to admit that the surplus-land problem is here to stay, the USDA now has initiated another program resembling the Soil Bank, also for ten years. Under the name of the new Conservation Reserve Program, signups started in 1985 and after a slow start reached a few million acres. Apparently, the program plans to reach some 45 million acres (USDA *Agricultural Outlook*, September 1986), perhaps by 1990.

This policy is ostensibly for soil conservation, but its immediate purpose is to place set-aside on a better basis. Unlike the present set-aside program, under which farms in all classes of land productivity set aside the same portion of their land, this program should at least differentiate, leaving the better lands in production more completely. They, too, may be the subject of annual set-aside, in case this new soil conservation reserve fails to curb the surplus sufficiently, as was the case with the old Soil Bank, which took mainly low productive lands.

The physical and economic needs for soil and water conservation are another subject. It remains to be seen whether the continued use of all U.S. farmland is needed to feed this nation, let alone the rest of the world.

WHAT IF WE EAT LESS MEAT?

The statistics seem to show that of the entire cropland base, only about two-thirds are actually used for crops, and, of that, one-third is used for crops to be exported. That leaves about 225 million acres of cropland to serve domestic needs, complemented by the vast pastureland on which cattle and sheep are grazing. In all the projections of future needs for agricultural land, the assumption has been that U.S. people would continue eating as they have in the recent past. This means a large component of meat—beef, pork, lamb, and poultry. Direct food crops occupy only a minor part of U.S. cropland. Most of it produces meat, directly or indirectly.

Continued high level of meat consumption is by no means to be taken for granted. Already consumption is tending to shift within the meat complex, away from the expensive red meats and toward the less expensive poultry meats, which are being marketed in more and more varied forms. On the horizon there are also new foods, imitation meats and others produced by intensive processing of crops, without a cycle of animal production. On the whole, they are much cheaper than real meat, and they require much less land to be produced. We already have an analogy in margarine, based largely on soybean oil, which has taken most of the market for table fat and caused a great decline in the use of land for dairy farming. Corn sweeteners also replace more and more of the market for sugar from beets and cane. If we are facing a breakthrough for high-protein foods based directly on crops, we may see some dramatic changes in land use and the economics of farming.

Many years ago, in connection with some food crisis abroad, a senior economist in the USDA said that if U.S. people would eat half as much meat as they do, 100 million tons of grain would be available for other uses. This would be the equivalent of 40 million acres in corn, somewhat more if other grains are also in the mix. By a large-scale transition from natural meat and milk, large parts of the cropland now feeding U.S. people could be freed up for other purposes—maybe as much as 100 million acres, leaving something between 100 and 150 million acres really serving current domestic needs for food and fiber crops.

Such a development, if not accompanied by new profitable land uses, would spell very hard times for U.S. farmers, and they meet this trend with undisguised hostility. In the early 1940s, farmer interest caused the Iowa State College of Agriculture to withdraw an extension publication that explained the merits of margarine in comparison with butter. Margarine's control of most of the table fat market has happened gradually without too much open conflict, but it is one of the background facts for the current surplus of land. With more butter from cows' milk, we would eat more completely what U.S. land can produce.

It should therefore not surprise us that farmers are very cool to the idea of "analogs" to replace meat. The USDA, after some wavering, declared that there was no great prospect to this kind of development because consumers would not want it. How can they want it if they are not exposed to it in full? The first line of defense for the meat interests was to begin producing and promoting meat with less fat content, lean meat, which certainly does not require less land to produce. As an extra defense for red meat, we are also told that large expanses of natural pastures can be used only if they serve as grazing for beef, especially young stock. Eliminate beef from the market, and there would be no use for these lands. Thus an important economy would be lost.

The argument, however, is not as strong as it seems. In many areas of the United States—especially those east of the Mississippi but many west of the river, too—the land being used as pasture is humid enough so that it could be used either as cropland or as forest, with fuel feedstock as an option in both cases. Only in those areas, largely in the Rocky Mountain regions and the western Great Plains, where the rainfall is too low to sustain crops or forests, is it true that ruminant grazing is the only feasible economic use of the land. On such lands, it might be possible to run sheep for wool, a fiber source that in recent years has been increasingly supplied by imports.

Thus there is no insurmountable reason why a transition to lower-cost, crop-based foods should not run its course as far as consumers will agree, under the demand-pull for more fuel feedstocks rather than the supply-push for surplus farmland.

A BALANCE SHEET FOR POSSIBLE LAND USE

As a first installment, fuel feedstock could easily be put in place on the land currently withheld from production—not the same acres, but their equivalent in locations where such use is particularly well indicated.

Subsequently, as a biomass-based fuel industry grows and comes of age it can begin to exercise its market demand on more land. The trade-off against exports could well release a large part of the land now producing for exports into fuel production for the domestic economy, thereby reducing and eventually eliminating the need to import petroleum. And sooner or later the supply of even better crop-based foods, whether called meat analogs or something else, would cause even larger acreages to be released from conventional crop farming and turned into fuel farming.

Of the 540 million acres that the NALS counted as actual and potential cropland, at least 300 million acres, maybe more, could eventually be turned into fuel farming. To this can be added some part of the pasturelands, whenever the demand for meat has become substantially reduced. These changes will not happen overnight or over a few years. In the meantime, if use of methanol and/or biomass-based gasoline were to develop faster than the supply of biomass-based methanol, the difference could be filled by methanol from coal. The combination of converging trends of economic change and technological solutions to match makes the balance sheet sketched here realistic.

6

BIOMASS PRODUCTION AS SOIL CONSERVATION

Soil conservation is one of those topics about which much is said but less is really being done. The dangers of erosion and of poisons in the subsoil and the groundwaters are often discussed in professional papers, official policy statements, and the popular press.

The topic is as ubiquitous as the proverbial apple pie. Everyone is for conservation and for protecting our heritage of soil and water. When costly measures to improve conditions are proposed, however, opinions and explanations become worlds apart. Many writers are deeply concerned about the worsening conditions of soil and water; others assure us that these matters are, on the whole, under control, so we should not worry. In part these divisions of opinion reflect differences in planning horizons and attitudes toward the future.

Our immediate concern is not so much with the magnitude of the soil conservation problem as such. Rather we are concerned with changes in soil conditions if one or the other solution regarding biomass fuel is adopted for large-scale production. Ethyl alcohol from grain has roused sharp controversies because large-scale production might mean intensified arable land use that would worsen soil erosion. Trees and grass for methanol production, we are going to argue, can have the opposite effect by stabilizing soils and by reducing the rates at which groundwaters are impaired by fertilizers or pesticides.

To place these contrasts in perspective we need first to clarify the soil and water quality problems, before either of the biomass fuel enterprises is adopted on any large scale. Thus we need to specify in broad terms the current erosion problem and the present groundwater problem. Further we should be familiar with groundwater quality as it is affected by agricultural production systems. Next we need to look at what is being done to encourage soil conservation and to mitigate groundwater impairment. Subsequently we should follow the debate about the effects that biomass-for-fuel farming is expected or alleged to have on the quality of soil and water.

SOIL EROSION

Soil can be eroded by water and by wind. When running water is at work, we can have sheet erosion, rill erosion, or gully erosion. The difference between sheet and gully erosion is that sheet erosion merely shaves away some of the topsoil without much affecting the shape of the surface. Gully erosion cuts deep scars into the face of the landscape and can at length play serious havoc with topography, ruining drainage systems and undermining trees and buildings. Rill erosion is in between—rills are very small rivulets, which may do no more than accelerate sheet erosion, but they can also start the kind of problem that eventually deteriorates into gully erosion.

Wind erosion is nearly always sheet erosion, but in its more extreme forms it may pile up large dunes of windblown materials, which in their way play havoc with the landscape as much as does gully erosion. There was a good deal of destructive wind erosion in the United States in the "dust bowl" episode on the Great Plains in the 1930s. The Soviet Union repeated the same experience during its "virgin lands" campaign of the 1950s. The former brought drifting dust to Washington; the latter sent it all the way to Bucharest in Rumania. In more trivial cases, one may find house interiors dusted over on a windy spring day in the Midwest. Crops can have their leaves lacerated by blowing sand.

Soil erosion is a very serious problem in many countries, especially those in the tropics and the desert belts. It is on the whole much less important in the United States. It is possible to exaggerate it, and some exaggeration occurs in the literature. Among other things it is hardly correct to sum together the amounts of soil that are lost to all eroded fields and call that a soil loss for the country. Most of the outwash from both water and wind erosion settles somewhere else on land; only a minor portion reaches the sea. Some of the settling soil becomes a nuisance in drainage ditches and water reservoirs, but some becomes soil improvement on some other farmer's land. Wind erosion has even in some cases improved farmland by rendering the surface more level.

Loss of topsoil is in any event not the whole problem; sometimes it is hardly a problem at all. New soil is normally formed by the same natural processes that formed the soils we have. Especially when subsoils are deep, loss of some topsoil through a gradual process may remove no more than is being replaced. Natural soil formation is estimated to proceed at rates from two to five tons an acre each year. This means a soil sheet from one half millimeter to one millimeter thick. Erosion of four tons to five tons an acre each year will remove one inch of topsoil in about 25 years. In most situations this is acceptable, provided the process is sheet erosion and does not lead to the formation of gullies.

EROSION AND CONSERVATION IN THE UNITED STATES

The extent of soil erosion in the United States was estimated a few years ago (USDA *1980 Appraisal* 1981). The extent of soil loss through sheet and rill erosion was found from an equation containing values for rainfall and runoff, soil erodibility, length and steepness of slope, a cover and management value, and an erosion-control practice value. This covers sheet and rill erosion by water. For gully erosion there is no formula, nor is there any extent to which it can be accepted. It must be stopped, period.

The report shows that on the whole soil erosion is not very severe in the United States. There are regional and numerous local exceptions. Soil losses exceeding on the average five tons an acre are found in most of the lower Midwest where the rate of cropland use is high. Rates over five tons an acre also extend over most of the Southeast and the Middle Atlantic states. Rates between two tons and five tons are found in the Northeast, the lake states, and most of the plains, and a part of the Pacific Northwest. Soil losses below two tons an acre are found in most of the West, both the mountain areas and the Pacific states. Averages are shown in Figure 6.1.

Averages cover a great deal of variation. For instance, in the potato area of northeastern Maine, sloping croplands have lost 24 inches of soil on the average, over the years. There are also areas of serious erosion damage in the Pacific Northwest, in the plains states of Kansas and Nebraska, and in Iowa and Missouri.

Wind erosion is less easily measurable, and in most parts of the country a formula to account for it did not conform as well with the facts as did the water erosion formula. Other recent estimates of soil loss through erosion are shown in a special "Soil Degradation" report to the *National Agricultural Lands Study* (NALS 1981).

The federal government has for many years helped farmers who want to conserve their land against erosion. These measures take various forms, as loans or subsidies for conservation measures, some of which are also promoted by state agricultural departments.

The difficulty about such efforts at the level of individual farms is in the planning horizon of the individual. Many farmers find that they can earn higher incomes by putting on more fertilizers than by applying

Figure 6.1
Average Annual Cropland Erosion, 1982

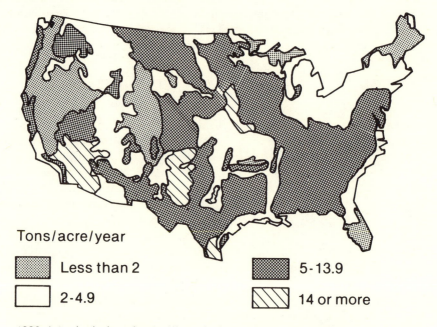

Tons/acre/year

Less than 2   5-13.9

2-4.9   14 or more

1982 data. Includes sheet, rill, and wind erosion on cropland.

Source: *1985 Agricultural Chart Book*, USDA Agricultural Handbook No. 652, Washington, D.C., 1986.

contour plowing, grassy waterways, or other measures to impede soil erosion (Ervin and Ervin 1982; Kramer et al. 1983; Collins and Headly 1983). Economic theory tends to agree. In strict actuarial terms, the future does not appear worth saving because the present value of a future income stream becomes too small 25 years from now for a present owner to consider.

This is the problem of "intertemporal choice." When it is reformulated as an intergenerational choice, the answer may differ depending on what attitudes generations have to each other. Some ethnic groups, which keep in some degree outside mainstream economic life, seem to be able to place a higher value on land ownership and the future quality of land. For most farmers it is a question of financial survival in their own time.

From the viewpoint of the national economy, the result of actuarial logic appears absurd. The nation must do something to preserve its resources so that future generations can have them as unimpaired as possible. The current soil conservation programs can be seen in this perspective, but generally they appear insufficient to counter the results of individual economic logic.

Instead, the federal government occasionally develops programs to attack the soil degradation problem in a more systematic way. One such attempt was the Soil Bank program of the 1950s, which was designed to meet the twin problems of surplus agricultural production and soil erosion. It did some good for conservation while the impact on surplus production was uncertain. The ten-year contracts generally expired about 1970, and when the grain boom of the mid–1970s came, there were only minor acreages that the Soil Bank had removed from cropland use—generally in locations where land use had been switched to forestry, maybe even in some national forest as in southern Illinois.

The grain boom of the 1970s focused attention on the soil problems, and the federal government now has a national program for soil and water conservation. Detailed studies have been done to establish the amount of soil loss under different cropping systems (English et al. 1982). Again, as in the 1950s, an initiative has been taken to combine soil conservation with the reduction of surplus production. The new Conservation Reserve Program started in January 1986. It aims at withdrawing eventually as much as 45 million acres of erodible cropland, on long-term contracts under which the federal government pays landowners the rental value of the land withdrawn from production.

A study done to prepare for this initiative showed that on 32 million acres of highly erodible cropland with soil losses averaging 20 tons a year, a program of idling this land could reduce erosion to one-tenth, that is to acceptable levels (Webb et al. 1986). Water erosion would be reduced by an aggregate of 600 million tons a year, and the federal government would save an estimated $5 billion a year in comparison with current programs for set-aside of cropland. The study showed that there would be some increase in prices of farm products when farmers were no longer producing on this erodible land.

Such programs do not address the whole erosion problem. The cited report focused on the 32 million acres on which annual soil losses were 20 tons an acre a year. Since the generally accepted tolerance limit is 5 tons, it follows that the lands having between 5 tons and 20 tons are a much larger area. It is certain to be much larger than the 13 million acres that are the difference between the reports' 32 million and the new conservation reserve's target of 45 million acres. How much more does not seem possible to estimate with the data at hand. It can be shown, in any event, that total marginal farmland is a much larger area than 45 million acres. A low point is represented by Illinois, where land in conservation use or in need of permanent cover or in need of sod in the rotation totals more than four million acres that should, to best advantage, be withdrawn from annual cropland use (Herendeen and Dovring 1984). This is about 15 percent of all the farmland in the state and a somewhat larger percentage of its cropland. The same percentage was found to vary between 17 percent, in Iowa, and 39 percent, in Michigan, among the Great Lakes states. Among themselves, these seven states (lake states and Corn Belt minus Missouri) were found to have 47 million acres of marginal land, or one-fourth of their farmland area (Campbell and Majerus, 1986b). It is obvious that if similar criteria had been applied to all the high-rainfall areas in the country, much more land than the 45 million acres in the new Conservation Reserve would be designated to need protection against erosion.

WATER POLLUTION AND THE FARMER

Poisons in the soil are yet another matter where more is said than done. Most of the pollution of groundwater and flowing water originates in industry or households; chemical factories and garbage dumps contribute more pollution than is currently being removed. The USDA *1980 Appraisal* also shows maps to indicate where streams have limited water quality in the conterminous United States. In the eastern half of the United States, over 20 percent of the streams in more than half of the areas have limited water quality; in several areas as much as 60 percent to 80 percent. There is also a good deal of limited water quality in the Northwest. The Southwest, by contrast, suffers from overdraft of groundwater for industrial, municipal, and agricultural uses (see Figure 6.2). The whole economy of the region may have overexpanded, and at least irrigation agriculture should contract in years to come.

Water pollution originating in industrial activity and garbage disposal does not directly affect our discussion here. Indirectly it may, to the extent that biomass fuel eventually leads to less pollution of all kinds. Certainly methanol as motor fuel will not bring any sulfur, and very few nitrates, to the atmosphere, so it should not contribute much to acid rain, which is one of the less tractable forms of soil poisoning. What concerns us here instead is how a change in cropping system, such as one or the other of the plausible biomass farming systems gaining momentum, would affect pollution.

The point can be anticipated because already the prevalence of different farming systems for food and fiber contributes different amounts of poisons to the soil as well as to soil erosion. Agriculture as a pollutant has come to attention in recent years because of the more and more intensive use of agricultural chemicals, both fertilizers and pesticides (Keene 1983). Both fertilizers and pesticides are spread over large areas so that in contrast to industrial pollution, which can be traced to some distinct source, agricultural pollution is often referred to as "nonpoint pollution" (Braden and Uchtmann 1985). Not all the washout from erosion is lost; some of it reaches other farmers' lands and brings some of the fertilizers with it. Some of the fertilizers and pesticides penetrate to

Figure 6.2
Major Areas of Groundwater Mining

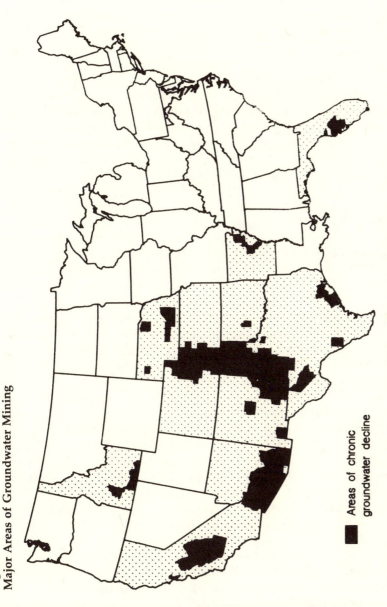

■ Areas of chronic
   groundwater decline

*Determinations were made by U.S. Geological Survey. Each of these 11 states has more than 500,000 acres in groundwater irrigation. Taken together, they account for 85 percent of the total U.S. area irrigated with groundwater.

*Source: Agricultural Resources, USDA, September 1987.

deeper layers where they may cause either temporary or permanent damage. When nitrogen fertilizers accumulate in groundwaters, for instance, these may become undrinkable.

The effect of biomass farming has been judged very differently depending on a program's emphasis.

ROW CROPS AND EROSION

Most of the attention to biomass fuels has been directed at ethanol made from corn, as a help to corn farmers and as an ingredient in gasohol. If gasohol leads to more corn production, how would this affect erosion? One of the early assessments was favorable. But it considered only a moderate amount of ethanol from corn, and it assumed that the DDG could be used in combination with roughage and would replace whole corn rather than cause any net increase in demand (Herman 1981a, 1981b).

With the opposite thrust, several writers have pointed out that if ethanol were to become an important element in this country's energy supply, the consequences of increased corn production could only worsen the problems of erosion and soil poisoning. More land in row crops would mean increased exposure to erosion because intertillage keeps the strips of land between the crop rows bare. Higher yields on the same corn land would require more fertilizers and more pesticides, which would lead to more of those substances escaping into the groundwaters and the subsoil. Farming for higher yields usually means higher costs at the margin. In the case of higher fertilizer intensity, this is even truer if the increase in intensity of application leads to more loss of fertilizers, as is usually true of nitrogen.

With large amounts of corn to be used for ethanol production, there would be so much more feed residue (DDG) that some of the soybean meal would be displaced. Thus, more corn would also lead to less soybean farming, meaning more fertilizer intensive farming. It would also mean more corn after corn, which in turn requires more pesticides to control the build-up of insect pests and nematodes that usually accompanies constant cropping with the same species. The issue reminds us that corn as an energy feedstock is very energy intensive and that additional corn grown specifically for energy may easily be even more so.

As far as they go, such comments have merit. It is less logical to use them as a way of downplaying the whole idea of biomass energy as an important option for the future (Pimentel et al. 1984). The same tendency was evident a few years ago in a book that tried to discredit biomass energy mainly on the basis of difficulties with ethanol; methanol was given very short shrift (Smil 1983). The erosion problem still appears to go unnoticed in some recent attempts to show high energy output from very high yielding corn (Klass 1987, citing work by Pasner et al. 1985). The same one-sided attention to ethanol dominates an even later overview book with ambitions to see into a future without oil (Gever et al. 1986).

The argument about row crops and erosion stands and falls with the ethanol alternative. It has no place in the discussion of methanol from biomass. The ethanol option is not rendered much better by assuming other grains as feedstocks. Wheat and barley are not row crops, but "close planted." The erosion hazard with them might be less and the net energy payoff larger because these crops are somewhat less energy intensive than corn. But the yield per area unit is considerably lower, so the prospect of large energy quantities from cropland is less evident.

CROP RESIDUES FROM THE FIELDS

Minor residues from crop processing such as citrus rinds are no problem for soil conservation, but neither are they any large contribution to energy supply. The large quantities of residues out in the fields—corn stalks, sorghum stalks, and wheat straw—pose an opportunity for energy production and a concomitant problem of soil and fertility conservation.

Corn stover as a feedstock for producing ethanol received attention early on. The DOE report of 1959 showed that the energy payoff would be much larger if the stover were used to produce methanol instead. To date, all technologies for producing ethanol by fermentation from treated cellulose materials are low productive with high costs. The issue was regarded important enough still in 1985 to be the subject of a USDA publication (Heid 1985).

Apart from the energy payoff from treating the stover, there are two major problems. One is storage; the other is the effect on soil depletion and soil exposure to erosion.

Storage has been regarded as important because it has been assumed that stover would have to be a major feedstock at the processing plants that, in the case of ethanol production from cellulose, would have to be fairly large. This type of processing hardly lends itself to farm level operation. Unlike hay, which is harvested in summertime and baled after field drying, stover cannot be baled with safety. When it becomes available at the time of the corn harvest, it is usually soggy from fall weather, and so the bales might explode a month or two later. The stover would have to be stored in less compact form—large heaps in storage areas near the processing plants. The proposal to store it in windrows along the roadsides appears to ignore the prevailing weather conditions in the Corn Belt. There seems to be no good solution to the storage problem, as far as we contemplate processing stover into ethanol.

For methanol the problem would be quite different. The processes are much simpler; the case for small plants is much better. Moreover, such small local plants could use a variety of feedstocks, turning to stover only for a month or two in the fall when the stover can be obtained from nearby fields. As with other methanol feedstocks, the residues from stover processing could be returned to the fields from which the stover came. Only nitrogen fertilizer would be lost; the other plant nutrients would still be present in the ashes.

The soil erosion problem is common to all uses of stover. Residues such as corn stover serve as protection of the soil against erosion in the late fall, winter, and early spring, provided the land is not being fall plowed. Removing all or most of it would thus increase the erosion hazard. The amount of stover or straw that can safely be removed will vary from area to area. It depends on climate, terrain (slope), and soil characteristics. The problem remains important in proportion to how much erodible land remains in annual cropping. The more land that is withdrawn from annual cropping and placed in permanent vegetation such as grass or trees, the less land that is exposed to more erosion because of loss of stover. The less in annual crops, and specifically in row crops, the less will need the protection afforded by retaining a large part of the stover. The possible removal of stover from flat fields (gradient less than 2 percent) can be a larger part of the stover on such fields. But the reduced acreage in annual crops will also mean reduction in the production of such field crop residues; thus, the transition to more permanent vegetation reduces both the opportunity and the problem. It would reduce the problem more than the opportunity. This is an example to show that analysis of present conditions is of limited value when we are reasoning about a dynamic future.

FIELD CROPS FOR PERMANENT GROWTH

The simplest way to change from annual crops to less tillage intensive land use is to produce grasses or other crops with permanent growth habits for harvesting as hay or silage. Such a change could also be reversed to annual cropping with a minimum of arrangements.

Permanent or semipermanent crops will need less tillage, hence less of the erosion hazard associated with newly plowed fields or with row crops. The USDA FEDS (Firm Enterprise Data System) budgets, which include hay crops in several states, prorate costs of establishing the hay crop: they may be prorated over 4 years, 5 years, sometimes over 18 years. The budgets specify the intervals at which the land is plowed. The length of intervals depends in part on what species or combinations of species are planted. The number of years without tillage may well become one of the criteria for choosing a species.

There are many more species of crops with long intervals between tillage episodes to choose from than in the case of annual crops for biomass energy. A 1979 report lists 70 species recommended for field screening. Most but not all are grasses (Saterson et al. 1979, pp. 63–71). Many species were screened away for one or more regions in the country.

Crops with perennial growth habits affect soil and water conservation differently than do annual crops. Apart from the lessened exposure to both water and wind erosion, such transfer should lead to less use of fertilizers and pesticides and to proportionately less of both being lost through erosion.

The difference may be even greater in full-scale application of biomass farming than would result from analyses of recent experience with similar crops in conventional agriculture. In selecting varieties for field-scale production of livestock forage, agronomists pay much attention to the protein content of the hay or silage. Protein requires nitrogen fertilizers. Apart from dryland alfalfa, which does not need nitrogen fertilizers, protein-rich hay needs a good deal of nitrogen added to the soil. There should be less use of nitrogen fertilizers in a biomass farming system for energy, for here the agronomic selection and breeding of species, varieties, and strains should focus on carbohydrate content and possibly on minimizing protein. Use of other fertilizers—phosphate, potash, lime, and micronutrients—is less of a problem. In a decentralized system of methanol plants, all of these would still be present in the ashes and could be returned, at moderate cost, to the fields from which the crops came. The chemical form of the elements may require attention, as in the classical phosphate problem, which usually is handled by adding lime.

Pesticides are a different issue. Some multienniel biomass crops are able to exercise their own weed control. For instance, the Jerusalem artichoke (*Helianthus tuberosus*) under permanent growth develops a coherent canopy early enough in the growing season to shade out any weeds that start from seeds. Bypassing chemical weed control may become another criterion for the choice of species. Insecticides, miticides, and fungicides pose different problems and, again, the relation between pest growth and accumulation and the number of years between plowings is likely to become yet another criterion for choice of species and varieties.

These many choices cannot be made here. With time, some of them will become different from what they are in the light of the latest research findings of 1987.

Biomass crops for hay or silage will require less chemical fertilizer and pesticide than is used on the croplands that would be converted from conventional farm crops to biomass crops. Such lands without doubt become less subject to tillage and chemicals. Some lands currently used as permanent pasture under low intensive management may become somewhat more intensively used, but the precise choice of species and production system could minimize damage. Across the board, use intensity of farmland will be lower under biomass farming for methanol than under present production for export and stockfeed. The methanol-oriented production system would also compare favorably with any system aiming at ethanol from crops, which would continue to favor grains over hay or silage.

INTENSIVE SHORT-ROTATION TREE PRODUCTION

Between conventional forestry and conventional field cropping is growing very young trees and harvesting them very young in order to take advantage of high rates of growth early in their life cycle. Fast-growing species are planted in relatively dense rows and harvested by machines somewhat resembling those for harvesting agricultural row crops. The trees are allowed to restore themselves by coppicing (sprouting shoots from or near the stumps). There can be two, three, or four rounds of coppicing; thereafter, the stand must be replaced altogether, at which time the field might be deployed for other use if the outgoing stand were not satisfactory.

The concept of intensive silviculture is somewhat elastic. Originally it seems to have aimed at tree plants to be harvested when they were two or three years old, but more recently even ten-year-old stands have been included in the discussion about intensive silviculture. Obviously the harvesting techniques will be different with such differences in age of the trees.

The yields claimed for such plantations are substantial (Zeimetz 1979). It is not clear whether such yields are generally superior to those from high-yielding herbaceous perennials. There may not be a single best choice. In many cases one or the other alternative—a tree or a grass—may be superior depending on many characteristics of the site.

Apart from the problem of establishing the entire stands at the same time without suffering losses causing lacunas in the tree rows, there is the problem of soil erosion. Tree plants in straight lines, with weed control in between and with heavy harvesting equipment driving on some of those unprotected strips of soil, might seem to conjure up some of the same erosion problems that attend row crops such as corn, sorghum, and soybeans. However, the planting and harvesting would usually not occur every year, so the total erosion hazard might still be less than in the case of agricultural row crops (Meridian Corporation 1986, p. 48). The caveat belongs here, it seems, that tree plantings of such intensive types could be used with relative safety only on rather level lands (slopes not much over 2 percent). On somewhat more sloping lands, herbaceous perennials would appear safer.

The problems of maintaining soil fertility and not poisoning the soil are essentially the same as in the cases of agricultural crops and biomass crops. If the woody material from intensive silviculture is used to produce methanol in small decentralized plants, the possibility of returning the plant nutrients (other than nitrogen) would appear as feasible as with other biomass feedstocks.

CONVENTIONAL FORESTRY

Growing whole trees until their annual growth increment begins to decline is on the whole a less intensive use of land than either intensive silviculture or intensive production of herbaceous perennials. It can, however, be made much more high yielding than is usually associated with averages of existing forest stands, including the well run and the neglected, the latter very common in farm forests.

For erosion control, forest growth is usually rated high. In general it is assumed that forest production can be applied to sites with as much gradient as 30 percent. This is based on the routine experience of the past, when wood debris was left to rot on the ground, thereby affording some protection against water erosion much in the way that stover does in the farm fields. If all wood debris on the ground between the trees is removed to be used as fuel or as feedstock, erosion may be accelerated even in a forest. Some extreme examples can be seen in the tropics, for example, India, where villagers' intensive search for even small scraps of firewood had so depleted the soil surface of any protection that the soil was eroded away, leaving trees standing on their taproots ("pillar forest") until they fell over and were destroyed in one way or another. Some recent tendency in this country for forest corporations to harvest all the debris to use as fuel in sawmills or pulpmills may open similar dangers even if they are not as extreme as in the tropics.

Removing the debris also removes some of the plant nutrients that under previous circumstances would reenter the soil. In other words, the more intensively the forest stand is harvested for all its biomass content, the greater will be the need to replace the missing soil nutrients by adding chemical fertilizers. Ashes from methanol plants will help, but they may not provide the whole answer, especially not if some of the wood being removed was used for purposes other than methanol production.

The erosion hazard, evidently, would depend on slope and kind of soil and climate. Need of nutrient replacing would also be greater on land where the incidence of erosion was large.

A MORE BALANCED LAND-USE SYSTEM

The above has done no more than sketch general indications, nor should more be attempted in this connection. A biomass production system for energy feedstocks can be made so varied by changing the proportions among the three main types of land use—perennial herbaceous crops, intensive silviculture, and conventional forestry—and among the many species and varieties of each, that it offers the ingredients of a land-use system that can be much more balanced and stable than the current agricultural land-use system with its relentless drive for maximizing the output of a small number of important market crops.

The conventional agricultural production system will generally be left in place on the best lands for agricultural production, "best" being defined by several criteria among which innate fertility is only one. Some of the lands in the plains states can be as profitable under relatively low-yielding crops as their counterparts in the Corn Belt with much higher yield potential. This depends both on the relation between crop yields and the need for fertilizers to raise them (if this is at all possible) and on possible alternative land uses. West of the hundredth meridian, there is less of a case for fast-growing species except under irrigation, which we will generally disregard as being too costly for fuel feedstock farming. The southwest may have to reduce its overexpanded agricultural system because of impending water shortages. But the Great Plains from North Dakota to Texas may be relatively less touched by the transition to large-scale biomass-for-fuel production than the eastern parts of the United States.

7

METHANOL RAW MATERIALS: POSSIBLE SUPPLIES AND COSTS

In some of the preceding chapters we have referred to various estimates of biomass being produced in this country—by nature and by organized agriculture and forestry. These estimates have in general been rather pessimistic in the sense that they would allow only modest contributions from biomass to the total national energy budget. Such low estimates have continued to appear in the literature until recently (Young et al. 1986). One reason for these kinds of estimates being low is that they generally reflect static assumptions about land productivity and land use. Biomass for fuel is allowed only a small residual after conventional claims have been met, as if nothing were to change.

In this chapter we shall sketch an entirely different scenario. First we shall discuss overall tonnages that may be required. Based on the discussions in Chapters 5 and 6, we expect that biomass production could already now occupy quite large acreages, eventually to become very large. To these acreages we should apply known findings about gross biomass yields of various species of perennial herbaceous crops, trees for intensive silviculture, and trees for conventional forestry.

Tonnages of biomass output are in themselves only gross figures. They need to be combined with conversion factors showing how much methanol could be produced from a ton or a metric ton of dry biomass. We will further need information about energy costs, labor costs, and total dollar costs with their distribution among labor, energy goods, and other material inputs for the production of biomass. This will give the background for the discussion in Chapter 8 about total costs for methanol from biomass.

We also need to compare costs and returns in biomass farming with those in conventional crop farming to be able to anticipate what the changeover to farming for fuel may mean for the farming industry and its operators, the individual farmers. Finally, costs of biomass farming should also be compared with current costs of federal farm supports, both those for present set-aside programs and those for the just initiated Conservation Reserve Program, as well as those for any continued set-aside programs that may still be necessary whenever the conservation reserve has reached its intended scope.

By these means we intend to trace the costs of a fuel feedstock program from biomass, to be compared with the costs of acquiring the feedstock for petroleum-derived fuels, which is crude oil, and other fossil fuel sources. In making this kind of comparison we need to keep in mind that in the future, costs of crude oil are likely to go up while those for biomass may stay the same or drop slowly. How the costs of processing—or, shall we say, refining—biomass feedstocks compare with those of processing fossil fuels and how the total costs of both groups of road fuel compare now and in the foreseeable future will be discussed in Chapter 8.

OVERALL QUANTITY REQUIREMENTS

Data from recent years indicate an annual consumption in the United States of about 100 billion gallons of motor gasoline and of about 40 billion gallons of diesel fuel. Using the conversion factors of 125,100 Btu per gallon of gasoline and 138,300 per gallon of diesel fuel, we obtain approximately 18 quads (quadrillion or 10^{15} Btu). This is somewhat more than one-fourth the annual energy budget of the United States, which is about 70 quads to 75 quads. When motor oil and jet fuel are included, total direct energy consumption in transportation in the United States is given as 19.5 quads in 1985.

The total drain of transportation on the national energy budget is considerably larger because of indirect energy used in production and refining of crude oil and in making and supplying all sorts of inputs to equipment and so on. This enlarged concept of energy requirement will not occupy us in the first place, but it must be kept in mind as we examine the indirect costs of biomass fuel.

How much biomass would it take to replace 18 quads of liquid road fuels with methanol? A gallon of methanol has a heat value (enthalpy) of about 65,000 Btu. Because it burns more efficiently than petroleum-based fuels, it actually replaces 78,000 Btu of gasoline or diesel fuel. Dividing the 18 quads by 78,000, we obtain 231 billion gallons of methanol. By the usual conversion factors of 185 gallons of methanol from a metric ton or 165 gallons from a (short) ton, we would need 1.25 billion metric tons or 1.40 billion short tons of dry biomass to replace the liquid road fuels. The conversion factors may be slightly different according to species and technique of harvesting, but these differences need not occupy us here.

It does not follow, because we compute this figure, that all of it will eventually be produced and used for direct road fuel. The logic of a switch of this kind also implies the possibility that a substantially smaller amount may be in demand by the time the switch is completed. Here, however, we will discuss the above finding of 1.25 billion metric tons or 1.40 billion tons.

Without anticipating the following exposition, we can establish certain ranges within which the land requirements may be found. If each acre produces four tons of biomass a year, which is not very ambitious, we would need 350 million acres to produce the 1.40 billion tons. At eight tons an acre, which is at present very ambitious but may well be reached in a medium-term future, the acreage requirements would be half, or 175 million acres. A halfway figure of six tons an acre, which may very well be reached within a decade, would leave us with a land requirement of 233 million acres. By the exposition in Chapter 5, this acreage could very well be made available to biomass production within two decades.

Comparing with the per acre unit estimates presented below, we should remember that an initial phase of biomass production for fuel will include mainly marginal land and that as the program matures it will increasingly come to take in use some of the better farmlands, which should help boost the possible average yields.

Moreover, methanol as road fuel may also be produced from materials other than those grown directly for this purpose. Omitting sewage and garbage, which may become earmarked more directly for municipal needs, at least some fraction of the corn stover and wheat straw should be available to augment the biomass feedstock grown for the purpose. There may also be some contribution from conventional forestry.

YIELDS OF HERBACEOUS PERENNIALS

Most herbaceous perennials are hay crops, and here we must not be misled by the yields of hay crops as reported in the current agricultural statistics. These are on the whole far below what can be obtained from carefully selected strains planted in the environments where they do best. For biomass fuel production, the leading criterion for selection of species and strains is not protein content, as is the case with hay for livestock feed, but maximum carbohydrate content.

Maximum reported yields of dry matter per area unit are the main data in a DOE report of 1979 (Saterson et al.). Disregarding the annuals, which sometimes yield very large quantities especially on irrigated land, species with perennial growth habits reach 4 tons to 6 tons an acre; some, much more: Bermuda grass in Georgia, with moderate water need, up to 12 tons an acre; orchard grass (*Dactylis glomerata*) and tall fescue (*Festuca arundinacea*), both in Indiana with medium water need (half as much as alfalfa) 7 tons an acre; alfalfa in California over 8.5 tons an acre, with moderate water need; blue panic grass (*Panicum antidotale*) in Arizona without irrigation, 8 tons an acre; switchgrass (*Panicum virgatum*) in Texas, with moderate water need, 10 tons an acre; and Reed canary grass (*Phalaris arundinacea*) in Indiana with moderate water need, 7.5 tons an acre.

Although these figures are given as maximum observed yield, this does not mean there are not higher yields observed elsewhere, outside the reports summarized in the above cited publication. For instance, the Eastern gama grass (*Tripsacum dactyloides*) is given here as having a maximum of 8 metric tons a hectare, or 3.6 tons an acre; no source is cited. A report from southern Illinois (*Update 80*) shows *Tripsacum* with 7.5 metric tons a hectare the year of establishment (which is always lower than other years), more than 24 tons in the second year, and more than 21 tons in the third year. Average of the three is 17.67 metric tons a hectare or almost 8 tons an acre. With longer-lasting stands, the average might be even higher. That is the highest-yielding grass in this Illinois report. The bluestems generally average about 12 metric tons a hectare or more than 5 tons an acre, but this average is downweighted by lower yields in the first year of each stand. Stands lasting more than three years might yield even more. The same reports also include variety trials with alfalfa, with production varying from four tons to seven tons an acre. These results are from southern Illinois, which does not have the best Corn Belt soils.

Another set of studies coordinated at the Oak Ridge National Laboratory includes experiments in Alabama, Virginia, Indiana, Ohio, and New York. For perennial hay crops, only first-year data are at hand (Cushman et al. 1987), so the yields are not yet representative of what is expected from subsequent years. Even so, Johnson grass at a southern location reached 10.8 dry metric tons a hectare (nearly 5 tons an acre) in the year of establishment. Based on conventional yield averages of 4 to 11 metric tons a hectare (1.8 tons to 5 tons per acre), the same yields are projected to rise toward 11 to 23 metric tons a hectare (5 to 10 tons an acre) by 1992 and 14 to 27 metric tons a hectare (6 to 12 tons an acre) by 2000 (Cushman et al. 1986, p. 42). Such yield projections assume continuing genetic and agronomic improvements.

CROPS FOR CRUDE OIL

Parallel with the search for biomass energy sources for liquid fuels from carbohydrates runs another line of inquiry and development with plants that contain crude oil or similar substances, ready to extract. These plants are particularly important in the arid areas of the U.S. Southwest. From the start the purpose of developing some of them for large-scale field production has been to combine the production of fuel with that of qualitatively important chemical feedstocks (Buchanan et al. 1980). A botanical inventory revealed about 200 species that could be considered for this kind of production (McLaughlin and Hoffman 1982).

This type of plant has potential as a chemical feedstock, but the rate of production to land and other resources does not appear to compare well with that of other biomass fuel feedstocks (McLaughlin et al. 1983; Hoffman 1985). One difficulty is that all these plants in the Southwest require irrigation, and the region already has overdrawn its water resources. As other data show both for grain crops and hay crops, irrigated production almost always costs more than rain fed production of the same crops. The argument has been made that the important aspect of the biocrude crops is not raw tonnage of biomass but the content of high-grade oils in the crops (McLaughlin et al. 1983). Even so the output of energy from these types of crops appears to compare only with that of hay or wood crops yielding two tons an acre (Hoffman 1985), a level of yield on which large-scale biomass fuel production could hardly be contemplated even in humid areas. All the land that might be used for biocrude production in the southwestern United States would produce little more than one quad of energy.

YIELDS OF INTENSIVE SILVICULTURE

"Intensive silviculture" is used interchangeably with expressions such as "short-rotation forestry." The concept includes the use of fast-growing, mostly deciduous woody species planted at close spacings and harvested over short time periods, from four years to ten years (Majerus 1986b; Meridian Corporation 1986). Sometimes, when fast-sprouting coppice or sucker vegetation yields the highest production in the first year, this type of crop is termed "wood grass."

Studies published by the Argonne National Laboratory of poplars and sycamores refer in part to rotations of 10 to 15 years (Vyas and Shen 1982). For poplars in the Great Lakes region, ten-year rotations with spacing four feet by four feet or eight feet by eight feet showed closely similar results, yielding 36 tons in ten years for initial growth and almost 40 tons in coppice growth. The former grew slowly at first and then accelerated; the coppice growth maintained a more even pace throughout the rotation period.

Sycamores in the South, in 15-year rotations, yielded from 73 tons to 75 tons over the rotation period, close to 5 tons an acre each year. The same difference between first growth and coppice growth was observed as with the poplars.

The same report has a study of poplars in the Pacific Northwest, a region with 200 frostfree days a year. Cuttings in the first year there could yield 25 tons an acre (wood grass). Maintaining the stand in a three-year rotation would result in 42 tons in three years, averaging 14 tons a year.

Further analysis of the same material favored the wood grass one-year coppice regrowth because of its high yield per acre (Shen et al. 1984). It was also emphasized that better harvest equipment would be needed to maximize this extremely short rotation.

A set of studies coordinated from the Tennessee Valley Authority at Oak Ridge gives data from several states (Ranney et al. 1985a, 1986a, 1987). Production per acre in short rotations is clearly related to climate. It varies from 3.2 tons an acre for hybrid poplars in Wisconsin to 8 tons an acre from eucalyptus in Hawaii. Pennsylvania and Kansas show intermediate results close to five tons an acre (poplars, cottonwood, and black locust), with pines and eucalyptus in Florida almost six tons an acre. Other details show that some of the highest results were obtained under irrigation, with up to 11 tons an acre a year of cottonwoods (Ranney et al. 1985b).

A recent report from the University of Illinois summarizes these and other results to say that in the Great Lakes region (lake states and most of the Corn Belt) yields are generally about 3.5 tons to 4 tons an acre (Majerus 1986b). Maximum yields of 9 tons to 13.5 tons are also mentioned in the same report. In subsequent cost estimates, yields from intensive silviculture are shown as varying between four tons and seven tons per acre (Campbell and Majerus 1986a).

For the Great Lakes region, a dozen species are indicated as promising. Among them are two nitrogen fixers, the black locust (*Robinia pseudacacia*), a leguminous tree, and the European alder (*Alnus glutinosa*), a nonlegume (Dawson 1979).

The foregoing results depend on careful management and the application of empirically found measures such as species and variety selection, weed control (which can mean twice the yield that is obtained without it), and soil management including fertilizers. The latter need not be applied every year but must be added at set intervals. There is empirical evidence, for example, from poplars, that wood yield can vary strongly with different levels of fertilizer application (Ranney et al. 1986a, p. 29). The possibility of recycling fertilizers from the ashes of methanol plants is not yet in the picture and will in time change the cost estimates.

The main limitation on the concept of intensive silviculture appears to be that it requires rather flat land. On sloping ground it would pose considerable erosion hazard, just as do agricultural row crops. Intensive silviculture is, in fact, a system of row crops. Even if the roots stay in the ground for several years running so that comprehensive tillage recurs only at longer intervals, the row operations for weed control and harvesting create some of the erosion hazards we associate with row cropping.

YIELDS OF CONVENTIONAL FORESTRY

Current statistics on forests and their production give the impression that forest lands are generally low productive; the annual average yield appears to be a mere fraction of a ton an acre. Such averages, however, are misleading. Detailed information on forest stands in different locations and under different management systems often differs greatly as to specific yields. The very lowest yields are, on the whole, on those 200 million acres of woodland included under land in farms. Farmers usually do not have the time or the inclination to pay much attention to their woodlands, especially if they were to produce by commercial forestry techniques.

An example of potential yield is given by the southern pines (loblolly and others). A long standing experiment in southern Illinois (a region where these species are close to their climatic limit) produced more than 2.5 tons an acre of timber; with the smaller tree parts, which are also usable for biomass, the total yield would come close to 5 tons an acre (Gilmore and Gregory 1974; Arnold 1978). These results are matched by more recent projections from the South, where future (year 2020) yields of biomass from pines is placed at 355 tons from 35 years of growth, of which 162 tons would remain on the site (roots, twigs and needles, and brush) while the total of usable biomass would be 193 tons, or 5.5 tons a year an acre over the 35 years (Koch 1980). This in turn would be divided among timber (a little over half) and wood of the kinds that may be used for biomass (a little less).

The example shows that, even though conventional forestry is likely to yield less an acre than either intensive silviculture or herbaceous perennials, the yields can be several times what has been usual. After all, conventional forestry usually occupies land not suitable for intensive silviculture, and it would yield inferior results in herbaceous crops if they could be grown there at all. In this perspective, the potential future yields from conventional forestry are likely to supply a substantial addition to biomass resources for fuel production.

Even if the outputs of conventional forestry continue to be claimed by the usual wood-using industries, as timber or as pulp for paper production, large parts of a tree are not ordinarily used in this way. Tops and branches represent somewhat less than half the weight of the tree, even without including twigs and falling leaves or needles. This potential contribution to biomass energy could be made even larger if the projections of genetic engineering in forest trees are realized.

A recent study of Douglas fir and loblolly pine in the South showed them to yield 2.6 tons and 1.6 tons an acre, respectively, in natural forest but as much as 4.4 tons and 6.4 tons, respectively, under intensive forest management (Trotter 1986). Even these yields could be more than doubled to 11 tons and 13½ tons an acre, respectively, if the author is realistic in projecting the results of future genetic engineering.

ENERGY COSTS OF BIOMASS CROPS

Because biomass crops are proposed as energy sources, it is important to know how much new energy they add. It is repeatedly argued that ethanol from corn is more of a vector for other energy sources than it is a source of new energy. (See Chapter 4.)

All energy production consumes some energy, and it is important to know how much. A recent article addressed this question for forest production, foremost from the standpoint of how the net/gross (N/G) ratio, or the energy ratio (energy out over energy in), may vary between tree production systems, specifically those of long and short rotations (Herendeen and Brown 1987). The rotations are all long ones, no wood grass. In general it was found that the shorter tree rotations are more energy efficient: they produce more new energy beyond what was spent in the production. Detailed specifications are given for hardwoods and for loblolly pine; fertilizer input is specified only for the latter. The N/G ratio is generally on the level of 0.97 to 0.98; the energy ratio is shown to vary from 52 to 61.

For our purpose the levels of ratios are more important than their variations between rotation systems. It is evident that in energy terms the woody raw material represents a large multiple of the energy input into forest production. However, these results do not include all costs of delivering the woody material to the processing plant.

Analysis of other recent studies (Herendeen and Brown 1987, p. 79) shows that some inputs can make a large difference. Especially if the wood has to be dried artificially, the energy ratio is lowered a good deal. This may not change the results in the article regarding the difference between different long rotations because solid timber is usually dried by leaving it in piles on the ground. It may make a difference in very short rotations; wood grass and other very short rotations in which the foliage is included among harvestable biomass may require artificial drying to be viable. Then the energy ratio becomes much lower.

For hay crops, the available material is less conclusive because it is based on hay production in conventional agriculture. Analyses based on the FEDS (Firm Enterprise Data System) for Midwestern states showed a comprehensive (direct plus indirect) energy cost of 800 Btu a pound of dry hay (Dovring 1984a). For alfalfa hay the cost was 900 Btu a pound, but this is influenced by irrigated production in Kansas and Nebraska. Such methods would hardly be recommended for biomass fuel production. In the same study 800 Btu a pound is considerably less than half the requirement for corn, which was 1,850 Btu a pound (about 100,000 a bushel).

When a ton of hay thus requires 1.6 million Btu and yields 165 gallons methanol of containing (65,000 Btu but able to replace 78,000 Btu worth of gasoline), the payoff in methanol is 10 3/4 million or nearly 13 million Btu, respectively, an energy ratio of 6 3/4 or 8. This is lower than for most cases of woody biomass, but the result for hay always means dry matter. Hay crops are nearly always sundried in the field before baling, whereas some kinds of woody biomass require artificial drying. The fuel ratio for hay is also a ratio for liquid fuel not just its biomass requirement.

The energy ratios for woody biomass as cited above refer, however, to the enthalpy of the wood. To compare with the ratios for hay-based methanol, the wood-based ratios will fall to about half.

RECYCLING THE ASHES

Plant nutrients absorbed by biomass crops could to a large extent be retrieved from ashes. The main exception would be nitrogen compounds, which are largely dissolved by burning or pyrolysis. Other nutrients might also to some extent be lost by attrition, but most of them should be available for recycling. To the extent this is so, long-term costs of biomass production could be reduced substantially. The reduction would be apparent on both the dollar and the energy-accounting levels, but it would be larger, relatively speaking, on the latter. Fertilizers are energy intensive goods, more so than production goods in general. Moreover, recycling has some costs, more important in dollar terms than in energy terms.

Recycling ashes was long neglected in the technical literature, more so than the topic of recycling agricultural wastes. A recent inquiry addressed the usefulness of wood ashes specifically as fertilizer on agricultural land (Naylor and Schmidt 1986). Wood ash samples were integrated into farmland soils at several levels of application (from 0 tons to 35.9 tons a hectare), and their chemical composition was compared with that of ground limestone, hydrated lime, and commercial potash fertilizer. These ashes contain considerable amounts of calcium and potassium and smaller amounts of phosphorus, magnesium, and a number of micronutrients. Not unexpectedly, it was found that such ashes can significantly replace commercial sources of potash fertilizer and liming materials.

The principle is clear enough in itself; it seems even more logical to apply ashes directly to the lands from which the biomass materials come in the first place. A logical part of a continuing biomass fuel production scheme would be for the processing plant of each kind of woody or herbaceous biomass feedstock to have standing contracts with the growers to return ashes to serve as fertilizers for continuing production of the same biomass crops. Forest production will at length have to obey the same law of replacing lost fertility as crop farming, and return of the ashes from the same crop would seem the most logical way to do this. Use of fertilizers other than ashes would not be eliminated, but it would be greatly reduced.

Whenever such recycling of ashes becomes generally applied, energy costs and dollar costs will be reduced. It will affect energy costs relatively more than dollar costs, because fertilizers are energy intensive goods, above average in this regard. Such recycling will improve the energy ratio considerably in nearly all cases because fertilizers represent a large part of all energy costs (direct and indirect) in most kinds of plant production. This is evident already in the short run with herbaceous crops. In the short run it may be less evident for woody plants, or so it may seem. Trees have deeper roots on the whole than herbaceous plants and so can draw on plant food in deeper layers of virgin soil. This is only temporary. At length the need to replace plant food removed with the crop will be basically the same for woody biomass as for all other crops.

DOLLAR COSTS OF BIOMASS

The Argonne studies on short-rotation forests also give break-even wood prices, assuming different harvesting costs and alternative discount rates varying from 0 percent to 20 percent (Vyas and Shen 1982; Shen et al. 1984). The higher percentage rates of interest would, however, occur only in times of rapid inflation, and then other prices would rise as well. Therefore the break-even prices connected with high interest rates are not comparable with those of low interest rates, which belong in times of slow or zero inflation. Comparable are only the real interest rates—the difference between current interest rates and the rates of inflation. We thus need consider only the break-even prices associated with interest rates up to 6 percent (at the most).

For a poplar plantation in the Great Lakes region we then obtain a range of break-even prices of $34 to $56 a ton; for sycamore in the South, $27 to $35; and for poplar plantation in the Pacific Northwest, $10 to $11.50 for 6 cuttings a square foot, but $23.50 to $25.50 at 2 cuttings a square foot. The former represents one-year rotation (wood grass) producing 25 dry tons an acre in a year; the latter reflects a yield of 9 dry tons an acre, also in a one-year rotation.

The studies of woody biomass production coordinated at Oak Ridge show costs per million Btu of biomass from those projects to be generally about twice the price of coal. This is at a discount rate of 6 percent, which is perhaps on the high side. More important, the price comparison relates only to the price of the fuel as it leaves the plantation or the mine. It does not account for the higher costs of coal beneficiation and scrubbing, which would raise the cost of coal considerably. Favorable transportation rates for coal also influence the comparison. The study concludes that woody biomass as an energy source is likely to become competitive with coal about the year 2000 (Ranney et al. 1986a). In energy terms, the cost of a million Btu varies from $2.90 to $5.10 for biomass, from $1.20 to $2.11 for coal depending on grade and location.

Carrying the same analysis a step further, the University of Illinois researchers found energy cost per million Btu from short-rotation forestry to vary from $1.51 to $2.93, depending on spacing, yield in the spacing, and level of coppice response (Campbell and Majerus 1986a). Average conditions would vary from $1.77 to $2.26, depending only on spacing.

For herbaceous perennials, there is as yet less research. The group at Oak Ridge has hypothesized yield and cost data relating to 1985 and 2000 (Cushman et al. 1987). The cost per million Btu ranges from $2.30 to $3.50 in 1985 and from $1.60 to $2.40 in 2000. This assumes grass yields from 4 tons to 8 dry tons an acre in 1985 and from 6 tons to 12 tons an acre in 2000. With much more detailed cost accounting, the University of Illinois researchers present costs for dry ton of grassy biomass from about $10 in the early 1970s to a range of about $25 to $37 in the late 1970s. These costs do not include land cost (Campbell and Majerus 1986a).

These ranges, and the varying assumptions included in the various cost estimates, do not allow a close comparison between woody and grassy biomass costs. But that is also not necessary. The two types of crops are not always competitive with each other; indeed, many species of each are also not competitive with each other. We have instead to expect that the pattern of land use will include many species, each planted in optimal environments. The general conclusion is that a large biomass-for-fuel farming system will include both trees and grasses, and that costs, within a decade or two, will become competitive with those of fossil energy sources, without bringing into account the long-range environmental consequences of unlimited use of fossil fuels.

DOLLAR COSTS AND FARM INCOME

The reverse of cost is income. Because we are proposing a switch of large parts of the farmland base to biomass production for fuel, we should also discuss the level of farmer income and landowner income per acre that may result from such changes in land use. How this relates to the incomes from land use in conventional farming must have some influence on the debate about our general proposal.

The gross figures are certainly impressive. The Argonne studies (Vyas and Shen 1982) combine yields and break-even prices to show gross turnover from about $125 to more than $200 an acre in poplar plantations in the Great Lakes region. For sycamore plantations in the South, we get a range from $160 to $180, and, in the Pacific Northwest poplar plantations, the range goes from about $215 to $260.

These cost figures can be compared with the sum of price times trend yield in each area and farm type. Such figures sometimes exceed those for costs but seldom by very large amounts, at least in the early 1980s. Data in the FEDS (Firm Enterprise Data System) crop budgets show wheat grossing about $100 to $150 an acre in the lakes region and about $200 in the Pacific Northwest on rainfed land ($300 on irrigated land, but that should not be contemplated here). High-value crops such as corn and soybeans in the central Corn Belt easily gross $300 to $400 an acre, but these lands are not comparable with those in the studies we are discussing here. If some of those lands were placed in biomass production, they would yield higher than the lands currently used for biomass production or experiments.

The studies on woody biomass coordinated at Oak Ridge generally suggest costs in the range of $300 to $400 an acre. These figures compare favorably with regular farm budget data from Pennsylvania, Kansas, and Wisconsin. Florida and Hawaii are more difficult to compare. These estimates generally include land costs as conventionally measured (contract rent).

Biomass from herbaceous perennials costs about $150 an acre for four tons of hay, without including land cost (Campbell and Majerus 1986a). This suggests that such crops may well be attractive in the areas and on the kinds of land where such yields are realistic. Better lands would now show higher yields. The land costs included in some of the calculations cited here are the same as for using the land for conventional agriculture; the cost estimates assume that landowners get the same level of income from owning the land as they do in conventional agriculture.

A critical point for farmers is labor cost, which also means labor income. Management is usually included at conventional levels, so that aspect of cost appears covered. In the cited studies, labor costs are not always identified separately from the operations to which they belong. We know, however, from the FEDS budgets that hay crops in general are somewhat more labor intensive than grain crops, principally because of harvest labor. Preharvest labor is less in hay crops because they are established only once in several years, but harvest labor is so much more that this alone forces labor cost—and labor income—higher. This is already so in the rather low-yielding hay crops shown in the FEDS budgets. For higher grass yields, leading to more cuts a year, the preponderance of direct labor would be even stronger.

The forestry data also do not consistently separate labor cost from the total cost of each operation in establishing, controlling weeds, and harvesting. However, it seems clear enough that intensive silviculture operations are relatively labor intensive, much more so than conventional forestry. Therefore the various forms of intensive biomass production, despite their lesser reliance on frequent tillage, will be able to generate farm operator and farm labor income on levels similar to those of conventional crop farming.

Crop farming has important forward linkages into animal husbandry, and to this extent the transition into biomass farming might appear as a loss of secondary intensity and hence employment in the whole farming industry. There will be important new opportunities for employment, however, both in transporting the biomass to factory and even more in operating the biomass fuel factories. In this connection it is of some importance that methanol plants can be built relatively small so that they can be widely dispersed among the farming areas where the feedstock is grown. Whether fixed or mobile, they should be able to supply additional employment to offset any loss in the animal husbandry sector.

SUBSIDIES FOR AN INFANT INDUSTRY

From the cost estimates cited above it becomes evident that biomass production for fuel feedstock may not always be competitive with other energy sources such as coal. Some varieties may be competitive already, but many are not yet. It is also clear that because of ongoing work in crop improvement and management systems, most, if not all, types of biomass fuel feedstock production will be competitive with fossil fuels about the year 2000, not much more than a decade from now. That will also be the time when the need for new fuel sources to replace the petroleum fuels, especially in road transportation, will begin to be critical. This is the classical case for subsidizing an infant industry: the industry cannot be willed into existence in short order, and the very subsidizing will allow the industry to grow more rapidly and gain experience leading toward higher productivity more quickly than can be expected under unsubsidized market conditions.

The magnitude of a plausible subsidy can be visualized without too much difficulty. Such a subsidy would never have to reach the levels of expenditure for current agricultural policy, which spends about $20 billion to $25 billion a year. The following is offered as an example of what may happen rather than as a definite plan.

Assume a program of 50 million acres in the near term, yielding on the average four tons of dry biomass an acre, at a cost of $60 a ton. This would mean 200 million tons of biomass at a cost of $12 billion. This is only half the current level of farm supports. But the subsidy would not have to be for the total cost of the biomass—rather, say half. This would leave the factory cost for the biomass at a level roughly competitive with the cost of coal. Toward the year 2000, we could think of 100 million acres in biomass crops, yielding six tons an acre on the average, at a cost averaging $40 a ton. This would mean a little over $2 per million Btu, which is already competitive with coal in many areas and close to it in others. Of the $24 billion worth of biomass, only a small fraction, if any, would have to be subsidized. Finally, toward the year 2010, we can envision 200 million acres in biomass production yielding eight tons an acre at a cost of $30 a ton. This would give us 1.6 billion tons, somewhat more than is needed to supply road fuel, at costs that would not need any subsidy.

The cost, or gross revenue, would be over one-third of recent farm sales (net of interfarm sales), which have totaled $160 billion to $165 billion. Net farm income is but a small fraction of this gross turnover. Biomass production would have a larger labor component in its cost account. The net farmer income from such production might well be closer to half that of the recent years, even though the 200 million acres are less than half the farm plant because biomass would initially occupy the least productive farmlands.

The current federal subsidies to agriculture are subsidies for nonuse of land for nonproduction. With our conventional agricultural system, there is no end in sight to this subsidizing of nonproduction. A subsidy to biomass fuel farming, by contrast, could cost much less than the current supports to conventional agriculture, and, in contrast to those subsidies, those to biomass fuel farming would end in time. Lowering costs will eventually allow the infant industry to grow up and meet its costs from regular market receipts. At the same time, a biomass production of the scope discussed here would remove the tendency for conventional agriculture to outproduce its markets. Conventional agriculture would also be able to survive without public subsidies.

The subsidies to farmers not to produce anything on part of their land are not a costless income. In order to receive the benefits from land withdrawal programs in the form of price guarantees, farmers must not only leave the set-aside land essentially unused (some grazing may be allowed after August 1); they must also spend money on soil conservation, on cover crops, and on harvesting the cover crops in such a way that they do not find their way to regular commodity markets. There are some hidden benefits in the system such as the provision of summer fallow on the northern plains (the Dakotas and Montana), which will increase yields next year, and the establishment of an alfalfa stand for hay production in subsequent years. With these provisos, famrers' costs for treating set-aside lands as the contracts require may range from $30 to $75 an acre, varying in part with the ways the farmers comply with the rules (Krenz and Garst 1985). At 50 million acres and an average of $40 an acre, these farmer outlays on nonproduction would seem to approach $2 billion a year in real costs.

NET COSTS OF BIOMASS FUEL FEEDSTOCK SYSTEMS

The real costs of a biomass-based fuel feedstock system cannot be gauged from observed costs in the present or the near-term future. Whereas biomass costs are certain to drop in the future, those of fossil sources can only rise. This is evident with petroleum as more and more expensive sources are called into service. In a short time, the same is going to happen with natural gas sources. Coal extraction may not be moving into more expensive sources to any large extent soon, but any large expansion in the use of coal will generate rising costs because of environmental protection and/or deterioration. The latter is a real cost, too.

The critical point to make, and it cannot be made too strongly, is that future reduction in the cost of biomass fuel feedstock production will come faster, the sooner such production is awarded a major role in the energy system. Conversely, continued reliance on fossil fuels as the mainstay of the energy system will delay research and development on biomass-based energy at all stages of production. If we follow only the signals of current market forces, we will continue on an upward trend of costs of fossil fuels until their cost level actually intersects that of biomass fuels. This intercept will be more delayed, the more the large-scale development of biomass fuel is delayed, and it will occur on a higher cost level, the longer the delay in biomasss development.

Comparing current supports for agriculture and subsidies to biomass fuel production, we sometimes hear the objection that farm supports are only money whereas biomass subsidies would reflect real costs. This is not quite correct. Idling farmland is a real opportunity cost. It is even accompanied by some outlays by farmers for cover crop. Costs of biomass fuel also regularly include the cost of land, which to some extent would be the land that is now held out of farm production against federal payments to farmers and landowners. The land cost is equally real in both cases. Shorn of land costs, the disadvantages of biomass fuel in the near term would be a good deal less than it appears when land costs are included.

More important is that the costs of agricultural supports lead us nowhere whereas subsidies to biomass fuel at the infant industry stage will

8

CONVERTING BIOMASS TO METHANOL

Methanol is often mentioned as the fuel of choice for future surface transportation. More and more, methanol is recognized as one of the most versatile fuels and basic chemicals. It is a fuel, a fuel precursor, and a raw material in many chemical processes (preface to Chang 1983). Methanol can be manufactured from several sources. Natural gas is only one of the sources from which methanol can be made. For convenience of handling, natural gas invites conversion to methanol because methanol is much less problematic for sea transportation. It is less volatile and harmless to marine life in case of a spill. Methanol is also less of a fire hazard; it does not spread as an oil spill, and a fire of burning methanol can be extinguished by water. Even over land, pipeline transportation of methanol is considered to be more economical than the same mode of transportation of natural gas over long distances, as from Alaska to the Midwest.

Methanol can also be used to produce gasoline. This is not without loss of energy content, but there can be situations where this is more convenient. The gasoline produced from methanol is free of sulfur.

The gas-to-methanol and the methanol-to-gasoline processes are both examples of the versatility of methanol, and they strengthen the case for methanol as a choice fuel for the future. A competing line of development is oil produced directly from biomass, without using methanol as an intermediate step. Technological uncertainties apart, this path appears less versatile and less ecologically benign than that of neat methanol to be used as a propulsion fuel, which also has greater effect than oil-based fuels.

Much of the argument will turn on the relative costs of the alternatives.

In addition to current money costs, which can change in ways that are hard to predict, we should also keep track of energy costs of the various alternatives, as these are more objectively at hand and less subject to variation because of changing economic conditions.

METHANOL CHEMISTRY

Methanol owes some of its versatility to its simple chemical structure, CH_3OH. Only methane gas, among the currently used fuels, has a still simpler molecule, CH_4, but then a gaseous fuel is less convenient on moving vehicles than a liquid one. Ethanol has a somewhat more complex molecule, CH_3CH_2OH, and the gasolines as well as other petroleum derivatives have even more complex molecular structures.

At present, the rather small volume of methanol used annually in this country (mainly made from natural gas, and to some extent imported) is mainly for chemical feedstock. Only a minor portion is used as fuel (Klass 1985). Some writers point out that we should prefer the term methanol to methyl alcohol or wood alcohol because reference to alcohol may lead some to use it as a liquor substitute. It is more toxic than ethyl alcohol and can have severe health consequences, largely because it dissolves slower in the body. Methanol is also chemically active, which means that it is corrosive on many materials, but this does not pose very severe obstacles to its use as an engine fuel. It becomes a matter of which materials to use in the engine (Marsden 1983).

Producing methanol from biomass or coal, by way of synthesis gas, is a variation of the coal liquefaction techniques, which have been known since the German war efforts of the 1930s and early 1940s. The step of turning gas into liquid fuel by methanol synthesis involves the meeting of carbon monoxide, CO, and hydrogen gas. The carbon and the hydrogen are obtained from the gas to be synthesized, while the oxygen may be obtained from the same or from another source. This liquefaction step is generally thought of as standard technology and relatively free of problems. This does not prevent a still simpler process from being developed. The production of synthesis gas from biomass materials (cellulose, hemicellulose, and lignin) is still subject to much research along a number of technological alternatives. The criteria of choice so far appear to be mainly technological. On cost alone, choices would be more difficult to make at present because the several competing paths differ but moderately in cost (Beenackers and van Swaaij 1984).

Conversion of methane gas to methanol represents a sizable loss of energy potential (enthalpy). Against this stand the gains in versatility and ease of handling. Methanol is both easier to transport by sea and more convenient to use as a propulsion fuel than natural gas. The loss of energy potential when methanol is made from natural gas is in part recovered when the methanol is burned by a dissociation process. This is the methanol synthesis in reverse; it breaks the methanol molecule CH_3OH into $CO + 2H_2$, making hydrogen gas available for oxidation.

The loss of enthalpy is less striking in the case of methanol from synthesis gas, for here the gas mixture is only in part (usually a minor one) methane. Turning it all into methane (by methanation) would require further refinement steps not needed for methanol synthesis.

SYNTHESIS GAS PROCESSES

Techniques for obtaining methanol from wood have existed for some time, originally as a byproduct from charcoal making. In this technique, the yield of liquid fuel was very low; most of the feedstock went into charcoal. Patents for methanol from wood were made in Europe in the early 1900s. Although not very productive, this type of conversion was done before natural gas had been recognized as an important fuel. Research and development on methanol from biomass now goes on in many countries, among them Brazil, Canada, the European Economic Community, Sweden, and the United States.

Most processes for synthesis gas to be reformed into methanol include some partial combustion of the feedstock to provide much of the process heat in the plant. Such techniques of providing process heat from the feedstock are sometimes termed autothermal, contrasting with allothermal techniques where the heat is delivered from some other source such as electricity. It appears that the biomass feedstock is a cheaper source of heat than any other, and so the autothermal processes are likely to prevail (Beenackers and van Swaaij 1983; Macnaughton et al. 1984, pp. 237 ff.). The term pyrolysis is often applied, sometimes combined into hydropyrolysis. This partial pyrolysis is in some contrast to the complete pyrolysis of the traditional charcoal pyre. The term and the concept are now widely applied in this specialized use (Antal 1982). There is even a specialized journal dedicated to analytical and applied pyrolysis.

A basic problem is that in wood and other biomass, as well as in coal, the proportions between carbon and hydrogen are usually not the same as in liquid fuels. Most carbohydrates have less hydrogen than is needed, and the difference must be supplied from some other sources, usually water. This is so whether the intended product is an alcohol or an oil, and the problem is essentially the same as in liquefaction of coal. Only crops containing natural fats can serve directly as a basis for oil production from biomass without introducing additional hydrogen. Their total scope is limited. In most cases the hydrogen is obtained from water in the form of steam to activate the gasification process or by some other means. A proposal has been made to utilize oil-bearing crops as an ingredient in a mixture of biomass sources, so as to increase the hydrogen content of the blend, but the result is as yet conjectural (Chen et al. 1986).

There is a problem with wet feedstock. Heat is needed to remove the water from wet feedstock. This is usually noted as an additional energy cost, which is especially important for green biomass from intensive silviculture. But the moisture in the feedstock can also be treated as a resource; it is already heated and can reduce the cost of making steam from cold water. Such "mined water" could be made to serve in the processing plant, up to 35 percent moisture in the feedstock. Excess mined water could even be made useful elsewhere (Wentworth and Othmer 1982).

Once in the process, the H_2O which is to supply additional hydrogen for the synthesis gas must be broken into its component elements. This breakup of water molecules is an energy-consuming process, as unavoidably as H_2O is an outcome of combustion when carbohydrates are burned or digested. This "climb up the thermodynamic ladder" is one of the basic inefficiencies in the conversion of solid carbohydrates into liquid fuels. This process also requires considerable capital with dollar costs to match. The same problem also occurs in petroleum refining when heavy fractions (heavy oil varieties) are to be turned into gasoline. That process also needs added hydrogen.

Even so, heat is not all that is needed to obtain the desired chemical outcome. To direct chemical changes toward target products, catalysts are used to prompt specific chemical changes and serve again in further rounds of the same chemical change. Most catalysts are metals, often metal alloys that give large scope for variation both of combinations and of the proportions within each alloy. Without catalysts, gasification of biomass or coal would result in a rather useless mixture of chemicals. Among other things, excess oxygen, which must be expelled from the mixture, would too often leave as water, taking some of the hydrogen with it. One of the prime objects of biomass conversion research is to find catalysts that work efficiently in delivering the desired products and which have a long lifespan. Some catalysts become inactive relatively soon. Others last much longer, and some are believed to have virtually indefinite lifetimes (Mudge et al. 1985). From time to time new research claims to have found more efficient catalysts, leading to cost savings in both energy and money (for example, Haggin 1986, reporting on results from Brookhaven National Laboratory).

GASOLINE FROM METHANOL

Conversion of methanol to gasoline has been the object of substantial efforts of research and development, foremost from the Mobil Corporation (Chang 1983). The results show that methanol can be transformed to gasoline with a high octane number, at relatively low cost. The new technology from Mobil is said to have reached the stage where commercial application is possible. A commercial scale plant in New Zealand was under construction in 1983 and was completed in 1987. A demonstration unit is built in West Germany.

Conversion of methanol to hydrocarbons involves the elimination of oxygen from the CH_3OH. The process does not appear to be quite clear theoretically, but oxygen can be eliminated as CO, CO_2 or H_2O; it cannot be removed as O_2 for thermodynamic reasons (Chang 1983). Methanol containing some water improves the process. It reduces the cost (including the energy cost) of producing the methanol in the first place because anhydrous methanol requires some energy for distillation.

In general, the synthetic gasoline produced from methanol is identical in all important respects to ordinary high-octane gasoline (Chang 1983). It contains no sulfur and hence leads to less air pollution.

In any event, the conversion means some loss of energy content. And one may wonder why gasoline should be preferred when the future will call for a methanol-based transportation system. One answer is that this gasoline can serve as a transitional solution in regions that are not yet ready to switch to cars with engines built to burn methanol. Each region, we assume, would prefer to have only one fuel or the other; both at a time might be more expensive as well as less convenient.

This should be the rationale in New Zealand where a recently found natural-gas field is best exploited by turning the gas into methanol. The country may not yet be ready to convert to an entirely methanol-fueled car fleet, and they still may want to draw some supplies of conventional gasoline from abroad. With this relatively small and geographically closed market, a clear-cut choice may appear inconvenient in the near term. In the distant future, New Zealand will plan for a biomass-based system of transportation fuel, utilizing rising yields from the country's abundant forest resources (Palmer 1984). There may be analogous cases among regions in the United States although, for geographic reasons, the case will seldom be as clear as in New Zealand.

Another motive for making gasoline out of methanol may be in the petroleum industry's desire to retain as large a market share as possible for as long as possible. Such a motive is logical for a firm such as Mobil. In even bolder form, the same motive may underlie the efforts to produce oil, to be turned into gasoline and diesel fuel substitutes, directly from biomass without going through methanol as an intermediate step.

OIL FROM BIOMASS

Reforming synthesis gas into oil rather than methanol is analogous in biomass conversion and coal conversion. Among other things it uses different catalysts than those for methanol production. Recent results from research and development indicate that conversion to oil may be competitive with conversion to methanol, as far as we only regard the heat content of the end product. Some research even expects higher conversion efficiency than in methanol production, but on condition that parts of the biomass have higher hydrogen contents because they are oil-bearing plants (Chen et al. 1986). Combustion efficiency and effects on air pollution will still make a difference in favor of methanol.

A review of research to 1985, published in 1987, shows two comparisons between oil from wood and methanol from wood (Klass 1987, pp. 61, 62). The first comparison is between a methanol synthesis path and two oil-producing techniques—one from the Pittsburgh Energy Technology Center and one from the University of Waterloo in Canada, the latter designated as "flash pyrolysis." When the oil is compared with methanol, both the oil processes show higher conversion efficiency (percent of feedstock enthalpy in the liquid product) as well as lower dollar cost per unit of energy in the output product. But the oil in these cases is not directly usable as motor fuel; therefore, a direct comparison with methanol is misleading. Like crude oil, such oil has to be refined to become transportation fuel. With refining into gasoline, thermal efficiency decreases and dollar costs per unit of energy rises so that both levels are close to those for methanol as a final product (the Pittsburgh process) or even worse (the Waterloo process). Methanol from wood converted into gasoline still fares worse than the oil-to-gasoline alternatives, but that follows already from the first round of results, and it would be relevant only if one insists on gasoline as the actual road fuel.

The other comparison (Klass 1987, p. 62) is between a methanol path, a diesel-fuel substitute from the Pittsburgh process, gasoline from the Mobil process, and transportation fuel from the old German Fischer-Tropsch technique of coal conversion here applied to wood liquefaction. In this comparison, methanol as end product comes close to the Pittsburgh process both for conversion efficiency and cost per energy unit, and it is better than the other two alternatives. The Fischer-Tropsch path comes out considerably worse than all the others, both for conversion efficiency and for cost per unit of energy in the fuel for final use. The Mobil process has to be somewhat behind the methanol-for-final-use path, because Mobil uses methanol as an intermediate step.

All of these comparisons are somewhat arbitrary as they involve conversion paths selected from among several alternatives. The results are also on the whole not yet plant-scale applications but have been determined by combining various partial results from laboratory studies and demonstration-scale plants.

As far as the results go, they do not recommend oil from biomass to be preferred over methanol from biomass. There are two main reasons.

For one thing, enthalpy of the end product is not all that counts. The propulsion effect must also be taken into account. Here methanol is better than the oil and gasoline alternatives because of methanol's recognized higher combustion efficiency in the engine.

In the above chapters we have reckoned with a 20 percent difference from the same heat units in the fuel's enthalpy, between methanol and gasoline. This estimate is used here and there in the literature. Estimates vary from 15 percent (Palmer 1984) up to 50 percent to 80 percent (Wentworth and Othmer 1982). It is not entirely clear what makes the estimates so different. It seems certain that the lower ranges, of 15 percent to 20 percent, do not include the effect of dissociation burning. When that is included, the advantage of methanol over gasoline is likely to be more than 20 percent. The authors proposing 50 percent to 80 percent also suggest that 1.3 gallons of methanol would replace one gallon of gasoline. Whatever percentage one is willing to accept, because of combustion efficiency methanol will be more productive even where its conversion efficiency is equal to or slightly less than some of the oil-from-biomass alternatives. The latter will have to show large technological improvements if they are to match the better methanol alternatives.

The other reason that methanol from biomass still appears superior to oil from biomass is the air pollution factor. Synthetic gasolines are free from sulfur and so are preferable to most conventional gasolines. But like conventional gassoline they are not only likely to produce less propulsion effect per unit of enthalpy than methanol because of lesser combustion efficiency. They are also likely to pollute the air more either by soot (particulate matter, unburned coal particles), or by high nitrate content in the exhaust, which is the usual consequence of raising combustion temperature to abate the soot problem by burning the carbon more completely. The now classical Los Angeles dilemma speaks in favor of the methanol alternative.

ENERGY BALANCES

All conversion from one energy good to another has some cost in energy. The transformed substance invariably has less energy content than the material from which it was made. Adding hydrogen and/or oxygen from other sources does not alter this invariant truth, for they too are obtained at some cost in energy. Yet many transformations bring gains in real terms if the output energy good is more useful or convenient than the input good or the bundle of input goods. The matter was discussed in Chapter 4 in connection with ethanol from crops. For methanol, the yield of high-grade fuel per unit of biomass used as feedstock is larger than with ethanol.

Two issues need to be discussed: how much does the process used affect the yield of methanol per ton of biomass feedstock? and how much energy other than the energy embodied in the feedstock is needed to produce the feedstock and to effect the transformation?

The first point is relatively simple. We have used as rules of thumb that a ton of dry biomass yields 165 gallons of methanol (or a metric ton yields 185 gallons) and that this means a conversion rate of about 50 percent. The ratio of output energy to feedstock energy is often referred to as "conversion efficiency" or "thermal efficiency."

These rules of thumb, with some variation, are roughly confirmed in the literature from recent research. In Klass's 1985 update (1987, p. 62), comparisons of four processes use an efficiency rating that is the heating value of the product divided by that of the feedstock. In this exposition, methanol from one process yields 56.8 percent of the feedstock energy as methanol; a variant of the Pittsburgh process (producing a diesel-fuel substitute) has a yield of 56.2 percent; the Mobil process (gasoline from methanol) is shown with 52.6 percent, and a transport fuel produced by the Fischer-Tropsch process yields 46.5 percent of the feedstock heat value as liquid fuel.

These are gross yields or gross conversion rates, for they reflect only the ratio of output fuel to input feedstock, without including among the inputs any other energy that may have been spent in the process. These other energy quantities are relatively modest in methanol production because the bulk of the process energy comes from the feedstock itself, the autothermal process referred to above. Yet these quantities of energy spent from other sources are far from negligible.

Ratios purporting to be more comprehensive, in adding external energy sources to the enthalpy of the feedstock before computing the proportion to the enthalpy of the output fuel, are shown in other tabulations as "thermal efficiency" (Klass 1985, p. 196), meaning total thermal energy in products and byproducts, divided by total energy input consumed in integrated plant. This ratio varies, among seven processes, from 43.4 to 52.9, with values over 50 in four of the seven cases. It is not entirely clear how the authors of the underlying reports define "total energy input consumed," but the reference to "in integrated plant" appears to mean that energy spent in growing the feedstock is not included and that other indirect energy costs are likely to be left out as well.

The amount of energy spent at various previous stages in production to deliver the inputs to the plant varies a great deal among kinds of energy goods. It is largest by far in the case of electricity, which requires about four times its own energy content to be produced. This indirect energy comes from all kinds of sources used in many parts of the economy.

At least one analysis of energy costs, both direct and indirect, dispels any such ambiguity (Hannon and Perez-Blanco 1979; Perez-Blanco and

Hannon 1982). In this study we are shown that the conversion ratio from wood to methanol (in the material cited by the authors) was about .53— one metric ton of methanol has an energy content of 22.23 GJ (gigajoule) or 21.17 million Btu. This becomes about 330 gallons of methanol, at 65,000 Btu per gallon. Such a yield comes from about two tons of wood. All the nonrenewable (commercial) energy quantities used in growing and delivering the wood and in operating the methanol plant are calculated at 9.8 GJ per metric ton of methanol. This lowers the overall conversion efficiency to about .43, not very far from some of the lower values among the more recent studies.

As the authors of the cited study point out, the energy cost of feedstock consumed in the process and the energy of nonrenewable fuels are not in the same category. In terms of nonrenewable fuel, methanol has a production efficiency of 2.3, meaning that energy output is that multiple of nonrenewable energy input. Thus methanol from wood delivers a substantial addition to available energy. This is in contrast both to methanol from natural gas and ethanol whether from crude oil or from corn. All have production efficiencies considerably below 1 and thus do not add to available energy. They rather subtract from it, and their production must be defended on use convenience alone.

Such increase in convenience occurs because the output energy good is more efficient, in the intended use, than the input energy goods, or at least some considerable part of them. In the case of ethanol from corn this advantage is not easy to demonstrate because much of the input energy in crop farming is either petroleum fuels or natural gas. To the extent the input energy bundle included electricity generated from burning coal, such increase in use efficiency also applies to methanol from whatever source it was produced.

The finding of a conversion efficiency of 2.3 can be discussed from several angles. It is specific to the methanol-producing processes that were available for study in the late 1970s, and some of these have been improved since then. No doubt more improvements will come. There are three major reasons that the real conversion efficiency could be viewed as considerably higher than the 2.3 found in the analysis. One is in the higher combustion efficiency of methanol. The others are in the requirements for distillation and for drying the wood.

The higher combustion efficiency has been taken into consideration above assuming a 20 percent higher propulsion effect would be realistic; it may well be even higher. Taking only the 20 percent estimate, the 2.3 conversion ratio rises to about 2.75, already a noteworthy improvement.

In the specification of energy costs (in terms of renewable energy) for methanol production in the cited study, the two largest items are for distillation and for production of the feedstock. Each amounts to about one-third of the nonrenewable energy cost. Distillation refers to the removal of water from the somewhat hydrous methanol, a product of the methanol synthesis. This water content of methanol is not nearly so large as that in ethanol as it leaves the fermentation tank, but the last few percentage points of water are always the most expensive to remove. The distillation of methanol requires a sizable, but far from prohibitive, amount of energy for distillation. However, the requirement that methanol be water free may not always apply. It does apply to methanol as a chemical feedstock or to methanol as an ingredient in gasohol, the blend of gasoline and alcohol fuel. It does not apply when the methanol is to be converted into gasoline, in which case a little water is actually an advantage. The same may well be true of methanol to be used as a neat car fuel. In trials with neat ethanol in farm machines it was found that a few percentage points of water improved engine performance by steam pressure. If this holds for methanol as car fuel, we could remove 3 GJ from the energy input. The ratio of energy out to nonrenewable energy in would go from 2.3 to 3.1 (from 2.75 to 3.7 when the higher combustion efficiency is included).

The energy used for wood production is more complicated. Herendeen and Brown (1987) showed only about 2 percent of the heat content of the wood as external energy cost, but the amount rose considerably when the energy cost of drying the wood was included. This is a complicated issue. According to Wentworth and Othmer (1982) wet feedstock could be an advantage by supplying the water, both for hydrogen and process steam, from within the process. This gain may not compensate for the whole of drying cost outside the plant, but it appears likely that use of wet feedstock would mean some economy of external energy. Only continued research can show how much such a gain might be, but it should to some extent improve the ratio of energy out to nonrenewable energy in.

DOLLAR COSTS

We should pay attention to more than recent cost estimates of a new energy system such as methanol from biomass as a road fuel. The solar energy systems, biomass among them, are likely to experience falling costs per unit of energy delivered as research, development, and industrial experience accumulate. There will be an intersection between a falling cost curve for biomass fuels and a rising one for petroleum fuels. Nevertheless, we want to examine some of the recent estimates of costs of methanol from biomass to gauge how close we are to reaching a cost level for a biomass-based methanol industry that is competitive without subsidies or economic protection.

We discuss several sets of estimates in chronological order of their appearance in the literature, with the general caveat that the value of the dollar has fallen in the meantime. More important than the absolute level of each estimate is the proportions between estimates—the estimates of relative costs.

One of the early sets, dated 1978 but referring to 1980 dollars, gives the following costs per gallon of methanol (Wan 1978, p. 131):

from methane reforming, $0.65

from residual partial oxidation, $0.74

from K-T coal gasification, $0.75

from improved coal gasification, $0.66

from gasification of biomass, $.045 to $0.86.

The last set of estimates varies in part because of size of plant and in part because of price of feedstock.

The first four of these estimates come from an Exxon report; the last line is from MITRE Corporation. Both sets are dated 1977. In 1978, the selling price of methanol was $0.45, which the cited article updates to $0.53 for 1980. Apparently, biomass-based methanol was already within reach of becoming competitive. In the high estimate ($0.86) the cost of feedstock was $25.80 a ton and was half the total cost; the low estimate ($0.45) had feedstock cost at $10.40 a ton which was still almost 40 percent of total cost.

This was before the oil-price shock of 1979–1981. Subsequent writers give somewhat divergent results. One early estimate, in an otherwise very optimistic article, gives the cost of methanol as 50 cents a gallon, or $7.50 per million Btu, when the feedstock is assumed to be poor-quality coal or lignite (Wentworth and Othmer 1982). Writing in the same year, Goodrich (1983) compares the cost of gasoline from imported crude oil with several alternatives of synthetic fuels for 1990 in 1981 prices. The gasoline from imported crude oil (the oil price at $32.50 a barrel) came to $1.27; gasoline from shale oil and coal came to much higher costs, from $1.75 to $2.85. Methanol from coal is estimated at 45 cents to 80 cents a gallon; methanol from biomass, at $0.80 to $1.65; and ethanol from biomass, at $1.15 to $1.90. When the higher combustion efficiency of methanol is included, the methanol prices can be revised (in gasoline equivalent) to a range of $1.30 to $1.30, and of $1.15 to $2.75, respectively. Evidently, in this comparison methanol leads the other synthetic fuels. In this version, methanol from coal is already competitive with gasoline from petroleum.

At about the same time two European writers, summarizing several projects, arrived at cost estimates for methanol varying from $0.83 to $1.01 per gallon (Beenackers and van Swaaij 1984). With an apparent cost spread of only about 20 percent, this variation was not deemed significant because of technological uncertainties. Instead, the simplest and most reliable process was thought most likely to proceed to large-scale application.

Two updates for the United States, for 1983 and 1985, also give some cost estimates (Klass 1985, 1987). The former of these (Klass 1985, p. 196) shows costs varying from 23 cents to 31 cents a liter, or from $291 to $384 a metric ton of methanol. At 21.2 million Btu or 325 gallons a metric ton, this gives a cost range for methanol of $0.90 to $1.18, or $1.72 to $2.28 per standard gasoline gallon equivalent. Lowering this by one-fifth because of the higher propulsion value of methanol, we obtain an effective cost range of $1.37 to $1.84. The cost of feedstock in these examples is about one-fourth the total cost. Thus a doubling of the price of feedstock would raise total cost by one-fourth; a reduction of the feedstock price by one-half would lower total cost by 12 percent to 13 percent. Capital charges are shown as larger than feedstock cost, and they include return to equity; all are calculated in constant 1983 dollars.

The 1985 update (Klass 1987, p. 61) shows methanol from wood according to one process at $16.31 a GJ, thus $17.20 a million Btu, which makes $2.17 a gallon of gasoline equivalent, or $1.80 when the higher propulsion value of methanol is included. This is at a wood cost of $33 a wet ton (1984 dollars). The same update in a different set of comparisons shows methanol from wood at $10.90 a million Btu, which is a close second among four processes, the other ones not being methanol. On a direct heat content basis this makes the price of a gallon of gasoline equivalent $1.36, or $1.10 when allowance is made for propulsion value.

Another recent set of estimates comes from New Zealand where current plans include conversion of natural gas to methanol and then to gasoline; long-term outlook indicates methanol from wood. This is in a forest-rich country with large opportunities for improved wood yields from the timberlands (Palmer 1984). The cost estimates here are complicated by the assumption of cogeneration of electricity from process steam. At an assumed price of NZ$288.11 a ton of methanol (US$195.90), with feedstock being wood wastes, the estimates show a negative price for feedstock in a small plant (100 tons of fuel-grade methanol a day). A 1,000-tons-a-day plant has a substantial positive feedstock price—from NZ$58 to NZ$94 (US$39.50 to 63.85). This indicates large returns to size, in the size range shown in these calculations, and substantial profit in the larger size ranges.

All of these estimates generally include results from various experimental or pilot-scale plants, not from full-scale integrated operations. Thus the results are mainly indicative. Yet they all point to the conclusion that methanol from biomass is well under way to becoming competitive and is virtually certain to be so when petroleum prices again rise, as they certainly must in the 1990s.

SIZE AND SCALE OF OPERATION

Size of processing plants is subject to "economies of size," which depends on a single large indivisible element of investment becoming cheaper (per unit of output) as it becomes larger. (It is conceptually distinct from "economies of scale." Up to some point, larger plants have lower investment costs per unit of material treated, whether this is measured as tonnage of feedstock or tonnage of output. For biomass processing plants there is a countervailing force because the larger supply area needed to supply a larger plant leads to higher costs of transportation for the feedstock.

For coal processing plants this limitation does not have to apply, provided the plant is located near a mine (or group of mines) large enough to supply the plant to capacity over its normal lifespan, until the plant has to be scrapped because of increasing age leading to repairs that are more costly than the depreciation of a new plant. Obsolescence, both technical and economic, also tends to limit the useful life of many industrial installations. Authors who concentrate their attention on coal conversion tend to recommend very large plants (Wentworth and Othmer 1982).

For biomass plants, a rule of thumb has been proposed by which the cost of the plant increases less than proportionately to the size of the plant, but in proportion to an exponent of 0.6 on the capacity (the "six-tenths rule," Marsden 1983, p. 342). In natural terms this is written:

$$\text{Cost} = K \text{ times Capacity}^{0.6}$$
and in logarithms:
$$\log\text{Cost} = \log K \text{ plus } 0.6 \log\text{Capacity}.$$

K is a constant, whose value in each case depends on things such as technology applied, kind of feedstock used, and other incidental circumstances.

It stands to reason that there has to be an upper limit to size even with this formula. A limit of 3,000 metric tons of methanol a day (or twice that amount of feedstock) has been proposed; a lower limit ought to be a few hundred tons (Marsden 1983). The 3,000-ton limit is based on Swedish experience with natural gas-based plants. An earlier writer referring to biomass uses the range (in tons of feedstock) of 335 tons and 1,340 tons a day, with 2,000 tons a day of other feedstocks (Wan 1978). The New Zealand writer cited above uses extremes of 100 tons and 1,000 tons of methanol output a day (Palmer 1984). A digest of European experience relates to plant sizes of a few hundred to 1,000 tons of wood a day (Beenackers and van Swaaij 1983, 1984). The U.S. updates cite cases with a few hundred up to 1,000 tons of wood a day (Klass 1985, 1987).

With a working year of 330 days for a processing plant, 100 tons a day of output or 200 tons of feedstock means 66,000 tons a year. At a yield of four tons an acre, the supply area would be, at a minimum, about 16,000 acres or 25 square miles. For larger plant capacities, corresponding multiples would apply. If yield rises to eight tons, the supply areas would be half as large.

Size of supply area increases cost of transportation, not in proportion to area size but rather in proportion to length of radius of the area. The size of a circular area is in proportion to the square of the radius times 3.14 (the circular constant, or π). The distance from center to periphery in a 25-square-mile area is about 2.9 miles; in an area ten times as large, it is about 9.1 miles. The proportion between 2.9 and 9.1 is about the square root of ten. Any increase in area size increases the distances by a factor that is the square root of the proportion in which the area has increased.

The factors mentioned here apply to a compact producing area in which all the land grows biomass for fuel. Whenever land use is mixed, areas are diluted, and the needed supply area increases in inverse proportion to the share of biomass feedstock crops in the land-use pattern. With half the land in biomass crops, the supply area needs to be twice that for compact production, and so on. Use of crop refuse (stover and straw) in the harvest season would bring some reduction in the size of the needed supply area.

How these distances affect the trade-off against returns to size in the plant itself depends on freight rates and on costs of maintaining the road network if this is not financed by way of truck license fees. In that case the road cost is already included in the freight rates. Corporation forests, for instance, often do their own road maintenance across private property. Freight rates in owned fleets have to be calculated from labor costs, fuel costs, vehicle depreciation, and a share in administrative costs.

The need for processing plants to be small is mentioned occasionally in the literature. Several years ago, International Harvester of Chicago started a project to design plants small enough to be loaded on large trailer trucks or railroad trains, in which case the size of the supply area would be of much less significance. The project appears not to have been completed, apparently because of the general discouragement of biomass energy projects in the early 1980s. A parallel approach is in an attempt to build plants, for reforming natural gas into methanol, small enough to be floated on barges (Marsden 1983). The purpose of such plants would be to utilize offshore gas wells that otherwise could not be used. From other indications in the literature it appears that the two main phases of biomass methanol manufacturing, the production of synthesis gas from the biomass and the reforming of the gas into methanol, are about equal in their investment costs. Thus, if the gas reforming part can be built small enough for floating on a set of barges, the former part (the gasification plant) may also be amenable to rather small size and maybe even be made mobile.

Returns to scale is a different concept from returns to size. It relates not to the size of plant but to volume of activity when that can be varied independently of large fixed installations. In our context it would apply in case a corporation controlling several plants were to attain better economy for that reason. Economies of scale as well as to size can also be negative because of diseconomies when size or volume of activity becomes excessive. These are practical points to be explored empirically; there is no general theory to predict what size or scale will be preferable. The critical or optimal values vary from one industry to another.

INVESTMENT COST AND INDUSTRIAL STRATEGY

Costs of a full-scale system for producing methanol from biomass are as yet largely conjectural, but some quantitative pointers can be given.

Several of the reports cited above give indications of capital costs for plants of one size or another. These data are themselves not very precise, and only indicative conclusions can be drawn. It appears significant, in any event, that several of these cost estimates tend toward a value, for relatively small plants, of $100 million for 300 tons of output a day. This points to capital costs of $3 a gallon of annual capacity.

Applying this rough estimate to the projected future need of 231 billion gallons of methanol a year to fuel the entire road fleet in the United States, we arrive at a total investment, to be in place when such a system is complete, of approximately $700 billion.

It does not follow that annual investment, over a 20-year period would be about $35 billion. It would almost certainly be larger, because plants of this kind usually have a useful life of less than 20 years. Most of the reports cited above do not address this question directly; one mentions 15 years as a plausible life of the plant (Palmer 1984).

The estimated magnitude can be compared with some indications in the literature as to the share of capital costs in total production costs. Capital charges are sometimes shown as occupying about one-fourth of total costs (Klass 1985, p. 196). If annual costs are between 200 and 300 billion dollars, annual capital charges would then be in the range of 50 billion to 75 billion. This includes return to equity and financing, which is larger than the cost of purchasing and installing the equipment.

These magnitudes may not be unreasonable nor impossible to bear, in the light of past experience with the petroleum industry. In recent years that industry spent about $25 billion a year for building new refinery capacity, apparently to replace worn-out or obsolescent plants. Also in recent years, drilling for new finds of oil and gas in the United States has cost about $10 billion a year. This is for supplying only a part of the prospective oil and gas supply in the country—one-third of the oil is imported; another large part comes from wells found some time ago, often long ago. The comparable cost for a petroleum industry to supply all the oil in the United States, from resources such as those we now have within the country, would cost a good deal more than $35 billion a year. There is no reason to expect the cost of continuing the petroleum system to be any cheaper than supporting the system of methanol from biomass proposed here.

Quite to the contrary. Costs of the petroleum system can only go up, whereas the methanol system is likely to experience gradually falling costs. Thus the broad indications given here confirm that the methanol system in all likelihood will be practically feasible within a medium-term future.

The earlier the methanol system is started, the less costly it will be, and the less strain there will be in completing it within some limited time frame. This has nothing to do with taking advantage of inflation in connection with investments, as some writers propose (Wentworth and Othmer 1982). Such inflationary gains (because debt service becomes lighter with the passage of time) are real only at the level of firms and individuals; at the level of the national economy they are irrelevant. There, all costs are real costs, and the only defensible cost estimates are those in money of constant value. But this does not weaken the general arguments in favor of starting a road fuel system based on methanol from biomass (with some from coal and natural gas in the transition phase) as early as possible.

9

USING METHANOL IN VEHICLES

Methanol as a propulsion fuel in road vehicles is not new, and there is substantial experience from specialized use. The very first automobiles built with internal-combustion engines (as distinct from steam locomobiles) were powered by methanol, in this case a byproduct from charcoal making. Even though methanol was soon replaced by gasoline and diesel fuel in most road vehicles, methanol has long been used by racing cars such as those in the Indianapolis 500. In such use cost is a secondary consideration, with power and safety prime concerns.

The first efforts to find replacements for petroleum fuels were directed at synthetic oil products from coal, as in the German and South African coal conversion enterprises. The same focus prevailed also in the United States, from the late 1940s onward. It is only recently that alcohol fuels have gained more attention. Even though much of the early interest in alcohol fuels centered around ethanol because of its perceived promise as an outlet for farm crops, it soon became evident that for any large-scale application methanol would be preferred—because of the much larger resource base and because of superior performance.

Use of alcohol fuels is in one sense simpler than that of gasoline. There are many kinds and descriptions of gasoline but only one methanol and only one ethanol, regardless of the raw material (feedstock) used to produce the alcohol. Only water content (hydrous versus anhydrous alcohol) makes a difference.

Recent and current debate about alcohol fuels for road vehicles has offered a profusion of arguments for and against alcohols in general and methanol in particular. On the positive side, methanol has great advantages because of large effect (power output or mileage in relation to heat content of the fuel), cleaner emissions, low combustion temperature, less risk of explosion than gasoline, and fewer environmental hazards from fuel spills. Among major problems advanced in the debate are corrosiveness, toxicity, difficulties with cold start, emissions of unburnt methanol and aldehydes, and low visibility of flames when burning. Lesser problems include those with blended fuels, fumes that may accumulate in a badly ventilated garage, and the risk of confusing methanol with beverage alcohol.

Throughout, the debate has been complicated by a dual approach: whether to adjust the fuel to the engine or to adjust the engine to the fuel. Connected with this is the difficulty of obtaining really convincing comparisons between fuels and fuel combinations because the testing can be done in many different ways. Each fuel really needs its own engine, which should mean that the cost of each engine ought to be part of the comparison. To date, engines have been better adapted to gasoline than to methanol, which tends to skew the comparisons in favor of gasoline. The balance of many comparisons now points heavily in favor of methanol as the principal fuel for road vehicles in the future.

LIQUID FUELS, NOT GASES

There are practical reasons for a road fuel being a liquid instead of a gas. Otherwise the conversion of natural gas to methanol or gasoline would mean an unnecessary expense both of energy lost and of money or money's worth spent in the conversion. Compressed gases in strong metal bottles have been used for kitchen-stove fuel in some countries, but this has always been for small quantities, and the immobile situation of a kitchen stove renders the size and weight of a bottle full of compressed gas less cumbersome than in a moving vehicle. The risk of explosion is also greater with a compressed gas than with a liquid fuel (Flemming and Bechtold 1982). Liquefied petroleum gas (LPG) has also been proposed as a car fuel although with less convincing arguments than for methanol. European experience shows LPG engines to be little more efficient than gasoline engines and clearly inferior to methanol engines (Menrad et al. 1983). Liquefied natural gas (methane) has proven to be even more problematic to handle and is seldom advocated as a solution to the future automotive fuel problem.

Nonetheless, the American Gas Association made its voice heard in a recent Congressional hearing (U.S. Congress 1986a, pp. 137–47), claiming that natural gas should be considered as a parallel avenue for innovation in automotive fuels. In the same hearings, an Amoco spokesman (pp. 149–52) who tried to invalidate the methanol case on the grounds of price, also made the countervailing argument that natural gas, like petroleum, is a scarce natural resource and offers no solution to the problem of dwindling resources. Neither party mentioned the case of out-of-the-way gas wells that can best be utilized by way of conversion to methanol.

POWER OUTPUT

Higher power output from the energy content of methanol has been mentioned several times in the above chapters. It is also a consistent theme in most recent literature and other public comments. Estimates from engine tests vary depending on how the tests were conducted. They also seem to vary with the speed of operation; the advantage of methanol appears to be greater at higher speeds (Menrad et al. 1983). This advantage is consistent in relation to both gasoline and LPG. Methanol usually performs better also than ethanol, which is intermediate between methanol and gasoline.

Engine tests usually show a power advantage of methanol, which is less than the 20 percent assumed in the above chapters. Several writers, however, assume even higher percentages. One reason for these differences may be in the early state of the arts in building engines intended to burn methanol.

A further boost in power output from methanol may be in the offing from a technique called "dissociation burning," which was recently explored by a team working for Conoco (Yoon et al. 1985). This technique assumes neat methanol, with no gasoline or other fuel additives. Much of the research turns on the catalysts to use. The presence of some water in the methanol is a definite advantage for this technique because water may increase catalyst selectivity. Thus the distillation stage in the methanol production plant can be saved when methanol is to be used in this way. The relative efficiency gain by dissociation burning is shown to be 20 percent to 35 percent over combustion of neat methanol and 40 percent to 60 percent over gasoline. Thus the advantage of neat methanol combustion (without the dissociation effect) over gasoline is assumed on the order of 20 percent. The higher gains depend on recovery of waste heat (for fully endothermic dissociation) and, in relation to gasoline, on high compression and waste-heat recovery in vaporizing.

In a parallel development, a French research team has published results from producing hydrogen gas from methanol, by a variant of steam reforming, which yields more hydrogen than the dissociation burning. This is for general industrial uses, not specifically for automotive engines. These findings strengthen the general case for methanol as a highly versatile basic material.

The dissociation version of methanol combustion is as yet experimental, but it appears to hold great promise. In addition to delivering more power it should also produce even less pollution than direct methanol combustion. Some direct burning of methanol is required, in the start-up phase, but this should be but a small fraction of total fuel use. The technique is also applicable to gas turbines and fuel cells for electricity generation. It thus opens a perspective of many uses for hydrous methanol not needing the distillation phase in methanol manufacture.

CLEANER EXHAUST EMISSIONS

Like synthetic gasoline, methanol contains no sulfur. Unlike both gasoline and diesel fuel, methanol emits less carbon other than CO. There is much less soot (particulate matter) in methanol emissions because of more complete combustion. Methanol engines also emit fewer nitrates as a result of lower combustion temperature.

Burning methanol does emit some unburnt methanol and some aldehydes (mainly formaldehyde) in the exhaust. Aldehyde emissions tend to be twice those from gasoline, and emissions of unburnt methanol tend to be correlated with the aldehydes in methanol engines (Gabele et al. 1985). In large cities with high traffic density, according to Paul Rothberg, the emissions of unburnt methanol and aldehydes might approach but would hardly exceed the limits where they would begin to pose a health hazard to the population (U.S. Congress 1984, p. 13). The emissions of unburnt methanol and aldehydes would be almost entirely eliminated under dissociation burning.

On the balance of several considerations, the Environmental Protection Agency has gone on record as strongly recommending methanol over other automotive fuels (U.S. Congress 1986a, pp. 43–62). This recommendation is especially positive as regards city buses, which emit large amounts of soot from their diesel fuel. Methanol engine emissions, such as they are, also lead to less formation of ozone in the atmosphere, thus to less smog in all its varieties. This point was made forcefully by a representative of the South Coast Air Quality Management District, which includes the Los Angeles metropolitan area (U.S. Congress 1986a, pp. 69–77). In this area, 95 percent of all ozone precursors come from petroleum fuels, both in vehicles and stationary uses. This is also an area where air pollution has already begun to affect the economic location of industry (Hall 1985).

OTHER HAZARDS

In several ways, methanol is less dangerous than gasoline. Whereas a collision often turns the exploding gasoline tank into a flaming inferno, this usually does not happen with methanol because it is less volatile than gasoline. This is one of the reasons for use of methanol in racing cars, which often get into collisions and other accidents because of the high speeds. Methanol is also less of a fire hazard. It does not spread like an oil film, and burning methanol can be extinguished by water. Thus it is also less of a fire hazard when stored, in a private garage for instance.

Methanol also poses less of a different kind of hazard: when a ship full of fuel breaks up at sea and the fuel is spilled into the water. Time and again we have seen pictures of the nightmare of a large oil spill spreading over the water and eventually reaching a shore where sea birds and other wildlife get trapped in the sticky mess. Nothing of this sort will happen with methanol. Even though methanol in some concentration is toxic, it will dilute in water to low concentrations in a very short time.

Methanol, however, is toxic to the human body and not only when ingested—it breaks down in the blood much slower than ethanol—but also with prolonged skin contact, for instance. It must thus be handled with care, but this is nothing extraordinary in today's chemicalized living conditions. When stored in a garage, methanol will have to be in closed containers so that fumes do not fill the garage.

Another hazard is present when methanol burns. It is not so difficult to extinguish as a gasoline fire; it can be done with water. But the flames of burning methanol are pale, almost invisible, which poses a danger to the unwary. Some additive can be used to color the flames and make them visible. So far the main additive tried has been gasoline but other chemical (nonfuel) additives would also be used.

CORROSION

There has been much talk about methanol being corrosive and, therefore, leading to rapid deterioration of engines and other parts with which it comes into contact. This is an obstacle to methanol use in vehicles unless the problem is understood and appropriate technological remedies are applied. When methanol is only a minor additive to a gasoline blend, as in gasohol, an anticorrosion additive may also be needed, depending on the engine's design. When car engines are built for use with methanol, some of the materials in the fuel system have to be changed, some of the rubbers, for instance. But according to automotive expertise, the corrosiveness of methanol is not really a major problem. It is simply a matter of choosing the right materials for the engine. Methanol has been known for a long time, and its chemical properties have been well explored (U.S. Congress 1984, pp. 30, 33).

COLD START

One of the pervasive complaints against methanol as a car fuel is that a methanol-fueled engine has difficulty starting in low temperatures, that is below 50–60 degrees Fahrenheit (10–16 degrees centigrade). Several solutions are feasible, none of them representing exotic or unusual technology.

In old-fashioned etnas, alcohol fuel was ignited by starting with a small amount of gasoline in a special container to warm the contraption, whereafterthe alcohol would burn without difficulty. The most frequent solution at present to the cold-start problem is to blend in some gasoline, up to 15 percent, which will facilitate ignition in low temperatures. This 85:15 blend of methanol and gasoline is often referred to as neat methanol (U.S. Congress 1986a, passim) although it is not really that. It does not seem to be clear from the literature how far such blends could share the problem of "phase separation," which is often experienced when methanol is used in a gasohol blend. It appears that blending with gasoline will always require anhydrous methanol, with attendant consequences for energy use and cost of production in manufacture because of distillation.

Other approaches to the cold-start problem include special kinds of sparkplugs such as high-energy ignition systems (Menrad et al. 1983, p. 127). One such innovation was recently announced by Caterpillar (*Cat Folks* 36:13, July 11, 1986). According to this release, Caterpillar has worked on methanol- and ethanol-powered engines, to meet the situation when such engines may be needed to replace those intended for diesel fuel in tractors, dump trucks, and other heavy motorized equipment. Ethanol engines are specially geared to the market in Brazil where ethanol from sugar cane is a large element in national energy policy. But Caterpillar's long-term interest is said to be in methanol. The new engine type includes an ignition assist that uses "a continuously energized high temperature glow plug." A test vehicle was already working (1986) satisfactorily in a coal mine.

Some innovation of this kind will undoubtedly be needed for dissociation burning of methanol. This process works by recycling the engine's own exhaust heat and cannot do this until the engine has begun working. Hence the process will require some fuel, such as nondissociated methanol, to be burnt at the start. Because the dissociation technique works best on hydrous methanol, it probably cannot use either anhydrous methanol or gasoline for the start-up. Some special ignition system will be required.

ADJUST THE FUEL TO THE ENGINE

Neat methanol cannot be used in conventional engines built for gasoline or diesel fuel. To gain some inroads into the fuel markets, one approach has been to blend small quantities of methanol into gasoline, a variant of the gasohol blend containing ethyl alcohol. The octane-boosting effect is similar in both alcohol fuels. The advantage of methanol is the much lower price compared to ethanol. But unlike the ethanol-based version of gasohol, the methanol version presents several problems at blending rates as low as 5 percent methanol.

One problem is corrosion, which is handled by special anticorrosion additives. Another is phase separation in the presence of water: if the methanol separates from the gasoline it also burns separately, which does away with most of the advantages of the blend. It is not enough that the methanol is anhydrous as it leaves the factory. Even small amounts of water can cause this problem. Methanol easily absorbs water, as in pipeline transportation or by condensation moisture seeping into the engine.

Because of these and several other technical problems with methanol as an additive to gasoline, several car manufacturers warn that their warranties are not valid if the engine uses a methanol blended fuel. Those that conditionally maintain their warranty usually limit the m ethanol to 5 percent and require that a cosolvent be added, for instance, ethanol or one of the heavy alcohols.

All told, the use of methanol as an octane booster is very complicated if it is to work satisfactorily. Numerous consumer complaints about this type of fuel blend have been registered. Such complaints can lead to distrust of any type of gasohol.

ADJUST THE ENGINE TO THE FUEL

New engine models are needed for burning neat methanol, including blends with up to 15 percent gasoline. The difficulty is that once an engine is built specifically for methanol, it cannot function well on gasoline or diesel fuel.

Ford Motor Company, which has done much work to produce car engines capable of running on neat methanol (such as the Ford Escort model), now has a double approach: the FFV (flexible fuel vehicle) and the dedicated methanol engine, according to Donald R. Buist, Director, Automotive and Fuel Economy Office in Ford Motor Company (U.S. Congress 1986a, pp. 103–8).

The FFV is to be capable of running on either methanol or gasoline or any random mixture of these fuels. Adjustment of the fuel blend should take place automatically; there would be no need for the driver to do anything or even to know exactly what goes on. Otherwise the driver would need to have complete and reliable information about the fuel mix at each filling stop; and the blend could change if the tank were not empty of one fuel mix when another mix is added. The flexible fuel system relies on a fuel sensor, which will detect the exact composition of the fuel mixture. There will also have to be special control technologies that adjust engine operation accordingly.

Results from this line of work are said to be encouraging but not yet definitive in 1985. At least another four years of research and development are needed before a fully functioning flexible fuel engine could be produced on the assembly line.

The rationale for the flexible fuel approach is that it is believed necessary to bring methanol into the fuel markets in a significant way, breaking the deadlock of the current "chicken-and-egg" problem, which most observers perceive as the chief obstacle to a wide use of methanol in road vehicles.

Engines intended for burning near-neat methanol are already on the market. Ford has sold several hundred of these: most are used in California. It is generally realized that engine models such as this early adaptation to burning methanol, with gasoline as an additive to overcome the cold-start problem, do not do full justice to the potential of methanol as a road fuel of the future. The gasoline-burning engine has the benefits of many decades of technical improvements. The current concepts of the gasoline and diesel engines are, therefore, technologically mature. Methanol-burning engines, so far, are little more than ad-hoc modifications of the gasoline-burning engine. Continued research and development, incorporating a growing body of experience of using methanol-burning engines, will surely produce engines that will greatly exceed current efficiency. Experience from racing cars should also help as it is incorporated into the general store of engine technology.

When they become technologically mature, the methanol-burning engines are expected to have considerably longer life than gasoline engines (Wentworth and Othmer 1982, p. 33). If this bears out, we can here look forward to one more gain in energy efficiency because it takes energy also to build engines.

EMERGING MARKETS

In the United States at present, interest in methanol-powered cars is most evident in California. This is logical, for California has a problem of gasoline-generated smog, so bad that mountain scenery becomes concealed much of the time, as in the San Bernardino Valley. Attempts to reduce the amount of air pollution in this region force more industrial decentralization and, hence, higher costs of industrial production than would obtain if the air were cleaner (Hall 1985).

Even so, direct demand for methanol-burning cars does not emerge in any practical way from individual consumers. Individuals have too little power over the smog, individually, for any one of them to have a very strong motive to take on the added effort of entering a new system. The methanol system as yet is small and cannot offer as complete service as can the dominant, gasoline-based system-in-place.

Of the several hundred methanol-burning cars recently reported to be in use in this country—most of them Ford Escorts—most have been procured by the California Energy Commission for state and local agencies, and a substantial number are owned by the Bank of America (U.S. Congress 1986a, pp. 32–38). This illustrates the need for public intervention in order to start any large systemic change. The case of the Bank of America brings to mind the role of large business as part of the government system—to society's advantage, in this case.

In other parts of the United States, there are only sporadic departures toward using methanol-burning car engines. Most of the attention in other states is to the methanol-based gasohol.

Some other parts of the world may be farther ahead toward a comprehensive methanol-burning transportation system. This may not yet be evident in the number of methanol-burning cars actually in operation, but it may be true in terms of systems being planned for the medium-term future. This is certainly so in some countries in Europe such as Germany and Sweden. Brazil has a policy of burning neat ethanol, based on its abundant sugar cane potential, which may in time be supplemented from manioc, a high-starch crop with low fertilizer requirements. New Zealand has a national fuel policy that, for the time being, emphasizes synthetic gasoline made from natural gas-based methanol; for the longer-term future, methanol from wood is anticipated as the lasting solution.

In the United States, any market development must depend on public policy as illustrated at the state level in California. When the recent trend appears slow, it depends in no small measure on current federal government policy that emphasizes "market forces," without always making clear what these forces are or how they are supposed to work. Uncertain direction contributes to making any change slower than it might be in the presence of clear signals.

Technical expertise seems to favor large-scale fleet tests as the best means of furthering more rapid development of the methanol-fueled car (Marsden 1983, p. 347). This was the purpose in the proposed federal test fleet of methanol-burning cars, but this proposal does not find favor in the present administration.

The methanol system may be begun in California. A system for distribution of methanol for motor vehicles in the South Coast Air Basin was set out last year by a contracting firm working for the U.S. Department of Energy (Energy Research Abstracts 1986, 12/10, No. 20165, 20168). Blueprints are at hand, action is waiting for decisive cues.

According to a recent news release, Atlantic Richfield Company (ARCO) has concluded an agreement with the State of California (at the initiative of the California Energy Commission) to install a methanol pump at 25 of its retail gas stations in southern California by the end of 1988 (*Chemical Engineering*, June 22, 1987, p. 31).

10

THE ROAD NOT TAKEN

At a crossroads, we have some option as to where we want to go. An option exercised may also mean an option foreclosed; the road we did not take may not be open to us again, at least for some time. The matter becomes more complicated when issues are linked together in multiple ways so that change in one line of activity may be possible only on condition that some other activities are also changed. Separate, one-track analyses all too often show that change is impossible because they assume all else was supposed to stay as it is.

This book has set forth and made the case for a departure in economic policy that is bolder and more revolutionary than most such proposals: to base the future energy system of the United States to a large extent on methanol produced from biomass. The proposal has many facets, depends on linkages with many parts of the economy, and promises solutions to problems as seemingly separate as oil imports, farm surplus production, soil erosion, air pollution, and the possible degradation of the ecosphere through overheating of the atmosphere.

This chapter summarizes the case as it has been made in the previous chapters. We will also move a bit further by reflecting on the consequences of making or not making some or all of the choices proposed for this policy departure. Choose we must, for the paradox of technological progress is that some people trust its inherent force to change the world so much that they neglect the role of conscious human will in deciding where the technological changes will take us. It does not help to say that human ingenuity can solve all our problems, unless we apply ingenuity also to the choosing among the myriad alternatives that technology keeps bringing into existence.

THE CASE FOR METHANOL FROM BIOMASS

The case for change is positive but includes a negative case against each of several alternatives. The petroleum age was sketched in Chapter 2, with the reasons for its disappearance in the near future. This will happen in the United States earlier than in the rest of the world. The United States began earliest to tap its petroleum resources and did so with so much success that social waste was deliberately fostered as a means of securing profits from a resource that at first was seen as abundant and hence cheap (Dovring 1984b, Chapter 3). Rising costs of domestic petroleum and low likelihood of continued import sources now make continued reliance on petroleum fuels in this country both uncertain and, ultimately, uneconomical.

The cases against the other alternative energy sources were made in Chapter 3 and Chapter 4. Substitutes from oil shale and tar sands are more than likely at length to cost more than those from biomass, quite apart from apparent technological bottlenecks such as the use of water, which may preclude very large annual supplies from such sources. The case against coal—and against the hypothesized immense reserves of primal gas—is that if we continue to use any fund-resource hydrocarbons indefinitely and in larger and larger quantities, the atmosphere will be overheated by greenhouse effect and by continued overload of additional heat.

The case against nuclear power rests on several arguments. One is that nuclear power also would bring too much additional heat to the atmosphere if the nuclear establishment becomes very large. Another is that a large nuclear establishment in the role of energy mainstay will need so much control over persons that a free society would be called into question. There is also the yet unsolved problem of nuclear waste products, which would take on much larger proportions. As the road taken, a large nuclear establishment would prevent other alternatives from being considered again—both because once such an establishment is in place it occupies the whole scene and because the vested interest of those owning or working in the system demands the enterprise be preserved.

The case against gasohol from fermentation alcohol was made in Chapter 4. The quantity data here show that ethyl alcohol from crops in this country could never be a mainstay for energy, not even for road transportation. It would remain limited to replacing, at most, one-tenth of the petroleum fuels for such transportation. Even so, grain alcohol draws too much on energy sources that are already available and that could fill a large part of the need that gasohol is called to fill. The gasohol path turns out to be a blind alley.

The positive case for methanol is that it is more efficient as transportation fuel both by higher power output from the same energy content and from less pollution in the exhaust emissions. The case for methanol to be produced at length from biomass rather than from coal and other fund resources is that biomass is a flow resource that can be relied upon indefinitely. As a flow resource it does not add either carbon or heat to the atmosphere. When biomass energy can also be used as a radical solution to the problem of surplus agricultural production (Chapter 5) and to that of soil erosion (Chapter 6), the case becomes definitely more attractive than any of the alternatives.

The cost of methanol produced from coal is already competitive; only the investment base is lacking. Thus the methanol system could be given a start before the biomass-based system has grown to sufficient size. The costs of methanol produced from biomass are already now bearable if we consider only a part of the costs now incurred to pay farmers to produce nothing on part of their lands (Chapter 7 and Chapter 8). Supporting a biomass-based methanol industry as an infant industry for some limited time will cost less than the current agricultural support system and will accelerate progress toward a biomass-based methanol system that will be fully competitive with any other alternative and more attractive than most because it is more benign to the ecology.

The use of methanol fuel in cars has been shown to be feasible and to have positive benefits in more power and less pollution; the latter is extremely important in large urban areas (Chapter 9). Less risk of explosion and of the kind of damage to the environment that we associate with oil spills should be sufficient to offset the caveats about methanol as a toxic substance that must be handled with some care.

A CASE FOR RADICAL CHANGE

Instead of trying to tinker marginally with existing fuel and land-use systems, this proposal offers a perspective of sweeping change. Unlike several preceding analyses, which nearly always arrived at low estimates of biomass production potential, this book proposes that biomass-based fuel could become a mainstay, at least for road fuel, eventually maybe much more. Aviation fuel may be a distinct possibility.

The difference comes from applying dynamic instead of static analysis. The low estimates of biomass potential for fuel production were based on current production data that do not include the potential of high-yielding strains already in existence or the likely effects of further biological improvements made for biomass production. The low estimates also accepted the habitual food exports of this country as if they were necessary for both the exporter nation and the world. They further assumed the inherited food habits of Americans without taking note of changes already under way, let alone those that can be facilitated when the farm industry no longer has a vested interest in continuing all of its usual production.

With proper regard for biological improvements as well as improvements in the techniques of grass and tree production, output of biomass per area unit can be placed much higher than at present. When there are no objections either against cheaper food to be produced directly from crops or against retrenching food exports, whose rationale is increasingly doubtful, then the acreages that can be made available for biomass production are without doubt several times larger than has usually been assumed.

A CASE OF INTERACTING FORCES

Instead of treating energy, agricultural surplus production, soil erosion, and air pollution as separate problems, this book emphasizes their interconnections.

With biomass energy replacing oil imports, there will be less need to export farm products. Thus biomass production for fuel leads to release of more land for biomass production. With biomass production for fuel, there will be no need to support prices of farm products, for biomass production can use any land that may become surplus for conventional farm crops. There need then be no surplus production to depress the farmers' prices. Initially we need to support the biomass industry as an infant industry, but such support can remain below what is now bestowed upon conventional farm production. Such support for the infant industry can be reduced and eliminated over a not very long stretch of years, as the infant industry graduates into a mature and competitive industry.

Instead of conserving the soil by not using some of the land, biomass production can help conserve it—and on larger areas, too—by permanent vegetation of grasses and trees. Instead of tinkering with means to render gasoline somewhat less polluting, methanol offers a clean fuel, which may in the future be made even cleaner by dissociation burning. By land-use diversification, biomass production for conversion into liquid fuel permits more rapid transition to lower-cost foods of vegetable origin, without this type of rational change being detrimental to farmers. This in turn will release even more land into use for biomass production. Thus the interaction approach permits one policy to solve many problems. In net account, and over time, these interacting solutions taken together will not be as expensive as separate solutions for the several problems.

A FLEXIBLE CASE

Even though the case made here will have revolutionary effects on the whole fabric of the U.S. economy, it is a flexible case that allows several ways to phase in the changes.

We will not need to build up the production of biomass for fuel as rapidly as the fleet of road vehicles is switched to using methanol for fuel. If the latter transition is reasonably rapid, methanol from coal and from natural gas (in out-of-the-way places) can readily fill the difference between the demand for methanol fuel and its supply from biomass. This does not imply any need to go slow on biomass for fuel; it only means that the possible rate of expansion for biomass fuel and of its conversion industry need not pose any constraint on the rate of transition to methanol as a fuel in road vehicles, or in any other use.

Nor does any of this mean that the demand for methanol in road vehicles must perforce place any ceiling on future biomass fuel production. If, as seems plausible, biomass-based fuel supply will eventually exceed the demand from the fleet of road vehicles, then other uses stand ready to absorb any surplus of biomass-based methanol. In the first place it may find use in aviation where the lower rate of pollution would be beneficial. Next to that, both electricity generation and industrial power can use any surplus from biomass. Dissociation burning, even with steam reforming for higher hydrogen output, will fit large stationary uses as well as, or maybe better than, moving vehicles.

Investment in coal and gas processing facilities will have to be made with some plan for phase-out. Generally such plants have a limited life-span, and those built within the next few years are likely to be fully depreciated and ready to be scrapped well within the transition phase of two to three decades. Similarly, petroleum-refining capacity recently built or retrofitted with new equipment should also be able to serve out its useful life within a prolonged transition period. Investment policy, behind the next decade at the most, will have to be watched so that we are not constrained by large fixed investments to continue liquefying coal, for instance, longer than is needed or longer than is safe for the atmosphere, just because a large body of plants has been built and will be operable for many years.

THE COUNTERCASE OF MARKET FORCES

The national administration in 1987 emphasizes market forces rather than planned public policy intervention. It wants to limit federal involvement in energy development to a minimum—some basic research plus some token gestures mainly by way of exhortation. Results of any consequence should originate within the private sector, so federal policy keeps saying.

This faith in market forces in today's complex economy and society risks confusing these forces with concepts derived from the far simpler conditions existing when Adam Smith enunciated the principle of the "invisible hand" as the best guide for the economic processes. Today's market forces are in part quite visible. Anyone contemplating the splendid constitutional heritage that this country owes to the same period of the late 1700s might also remember the reflections of James Madison, maybe the foremost author of the U.S. Constitution, when he warned against the power of money over civil freedoms.

Some such reflections will fit well with the need to reevaluate economic policy as a whole after the rather low success rate of the last six to seven years (Dovring 1987d). Market forces today are of many magnitudes, some of them so large and concentrated that they become in effect a part of the government system. Vested interests can do a great deal to delay necessary changes. In many cases it would be disingenuous to blame them for doing so. The large industrial system that delivers energy to the U.S. economy has many features of infrastructure and general overheads, and replacing one system with another is not done easily or automatically.

In the case of transportation fuel the transition is complicated by the "chicken-and-egg" problem that has often been referred to in the debate about methanol fuel. Which comes first—a large supply of the new fuel or a large supply of cars capable of using it? Neither, it appears. The case for market forces to accomplish this kind of transition is weak— more so than usual with problems of this caliber because political events far away, over which this country has no control, can cause the price of petroleum to fluctuate violently at short notice. Even those who believe the methanol case to be strong enough to rely mainly on market forces as they exist admit the need for some federal guarantee against the vagaries of the petroleum market (Wentworth and Othmer 1982).

ENERGY POLICY: 1970s VERSUS 1980s

The matter of a national energy policy was effectively buried when the Paley Report was shelved by the incoming administration in 1953. Twenty years later the issue came back with a jolt because of the first oil price shock combined with the rather ineffectual Arab oil embargo against the United States. Public opinion was aroused, politicians began listening to various proposals, and some elements of a national energy policy were set forth. In the late 1970s, we even got a federal Department of Energy (DOE). What passed for national energy policy was a mixture of familiar elements: reinforcing the belief in nuclear power and some renewed research and development in coal conversion. This was before

Three Mile Island and Chernobyl and before the reports on acid rain began to be alarming. Vague references to solar energy were followed mainly by a rash of activity on solar panels for home heating and some tax credits for people who bought them.

Energy "conservation" (meaning more efficient use) also made some inroads during the energy planning period of the 1970s. This was above all visible in the manufacturing industry, which could "trim the fat" with relative ease. This led to optimism among economists about the effect of energy prices on conservation. Economists should have understood the difference between the marginal and the average; once the fat has been trimmed, further reductions in direct energy use in industry come at higher costs in capital and in indirect energy.

Transportation, the largest energy-using sector in the United States, responded much less to the appeals for conservation. Several moves toward recommending more use of mass transit generally had a defeatist tone and had very slight influence on the level of energy use. That the gasohol initiative, of replacing up to 10 percent of the gasoline with grain alcohol, could be hailed as a major departure is typical of the period.

The attempts to formulate national energy policy in the 1970s were hampered by a lack of overview and systematic thought, which was only to be expected after 20 years of almost completely neglecting the whole problem. This unimpressive outcome of the early attempts at energy policy was then, paradoxically, allowed to discredit the whole concept of a government-led change in the energy system of the economy. It gave seeming justification to the administration in 1981 when it decided to deemphasize energy problems and policy. The same line of thinking led to an emphasis on production, rather than conservation, of more oil and gas in the United States.

This productionist line has been emphatically contradicted by events of this decade, but any corresponding shift in government thought and policy is slow. The early 1980s even saw a proposal to dismantle the DOE. It was allowed to continue mainly as an agency to organize the supply of nuclear explosives to the armed forces. A federal corporation intended to backstop coal conversion and shale oil development was eventually scrapped. Even money for research and development on energy in general and on biomass in particular was severely reduced, most recently in connection with the Gramm-Rudman Act to balance the federal budget. The project of a federal test fleet of methanol-burning cars was also out of favor with the administration in 1986.

FORCE OF HABIT AND SYSTEM IN PLACE

Changing habits should not be considered unpleasant in the United States, which has long prided itself on having a rather large share of the world's technological dynamism. When many of our energy-using habits appear difficult to change, more is involved than force of habit. Clinging to some invariants in daily life may be understandable when so much else is changing so quickly. For transportation, the force of system-in-place is even more important than force of habit.

The high level of energy use in the United States, both per capita and in relation to real national product, is the result of two interlocking systems: housing and transportation. Outside these sectors the level of energy intensity in the U.S. economy is close to the norm in other industrial countries (Dovring 1981a. See Table 10.1).

If there could have been a breakthrough in transportation, making mass transit the mainstay and individual driving an auxiliary means, energy consumption would have been greatly reduced. This in turn would have slowed the depletion of domestic oil reserves and reduced the need for oil imports. Such a breakthrough would require altered trends in housing, emphasizing more concentrated dwellings in all new construction. Even that would take time before it could alter the transportation system. The existing housing inventory is a powerful brake on any system change in transportation.

If such a switch in housing and transportation could still be started, the future requirement for transportation fuel, from whatever source, would also be reduced. The need to accelerate development of a biomass-based fuel system would then be less urgent, and the biomass fuel system once developed would go further toward covering other energy needs outside the transportation sector.

Not much has been done to change the systems-in-place of transportation and housing. Sweeping changes in the tax laws have not affected the tax privilege of housing. The car system seems again to emphasize large vehicles such as station wagons, pickup trucks with covered cargo area, and campers. Such changes in size or model counter any improvements in the energy efficiency of car engines.

Thus we have had to sketch the whole program in this book without any anticipation of changes in the energy intensity of the transportation system. The lack of movement in the transportation and housing sectors and the strength of these systems-in-place only make it so much more urgent that something soon be done about national energy policy.

A TIME FRAME FOR DECISION

The need to do something about energy now appears to be given more attention by industry than by government. Several of the energy industries have made significant contributions to forward-looking work in these areas: ARCO on promoting methanol as a car fuel, Conoco on dissociation burning of methanol, and Mobil on conversion of methanol

Table 10.1
Consumption per Capita of Total Energy and of Motor Gasoline, Selected Countries and Years

Country	1970	1975	1980	1983	1985
a) Total energy, oil equivalent kilograms per capita.					
France	2639	2579	3032	2739	2809
Germany (W)	3556	3648	4009	3872	4024
Japan	2232	2435	2563	2441	2600
United Kingdom	3352	3315	3336	3349	3439
United States	7436	7199	7143	6514	6694
USSR	2842	3468	3816	4090	4292
WORLD	1202	1255	1320	1281	1321
b) Motor gasoline, kilograms per capita.					
France	246	301	316	330	322
Germany (W)	253	325	385	415	418
Japan	..	193	219	222	223
United Kingdom	257	281	332	332	339
United States	1211	1324	1269	1215	1232
USSR	180	238	248	253	240
WORLD	129	143	143	137	137

Source: *Energy Statistics Yearbook*, United Nations, 1982 and 1985.

to gasoline. Transportation industries also have made contributions to new technologies: Ford with methanol-burning car engines and Caterpillar on analogous engines for heavy vehicles, to mention only two of the most important ones. Such departures are not due to market forces in the sense of current or immediately impending consumer demand; instead they are planning by industry. Such planning can no doubt be made more consequential if it is guided by cues from the national government, to show what future policy could and should be.

Industry is also heard in the public policy debate on the need for energy policy, and not only in hearings before Congress as cited in the previous chapters. Such industrial voices range from an oil company spokesman declaring in the summer of 1986, "The crisis in energy is here now!" (Keplinger 1986), to recommendations for a synthetic fuels policy in late 1986 from the American Institute of Chemical Engineers (Sperhac et al. 1986), and on to a top petroleum executive in the spring of 1987 calling for a national energy debate (Murray 1987). Even more recently, yet another voice in the petroleum press regrets that rising U.S. oil imports "get attention but no action" (Crow 1987). Even the American Automobile Association has emphasized that time is of the essence (U.S. Congress 1986a, p. 84).

Apparently, the outgoing administration is less sensitive to the energy problem than many of the organized forces in the country who are calling for government to show the way. There are more energy initiatives in Congress, as the cited hearings exemplify. The House bill on methanol in the fall of 1986 was not enacted because of lack of action in the Senate, but it has been taken up again in 1987, with some modifications. As this is being written, the bill is pending.

At the same time there is another initiative in Congress to inject new life into the gasohol program by calling for measures to promote the use of ethyl alcohol, mainly from grain. The goal is for half the gasoline in the country to contain 10 percent ethanol by the early 1990s. This would take the equivalent of 2 billion bushels of corn. It is not clear how far such a proposal anticipates the various direct and indirect consequences of corn use for fuel on such a scale. As before, the gasohol initiative is supply driven, as a means of helping corn farmers in the Midwest. To some extent even the current methanol initiative is supply driven, to help the coal industry.

The many uncertainties regarding energy policy emphasize one elemental fact: we have not yet taken any road; we are still drifting toward the next energy crunch without any directions for action, let alone industry ready to step in and replace oil. The administrations starting in 1953 and 1981 postponed and downplayed any future change in energy systems, and we are still burdened with the negative outcome of those policy decisions: no road leading to the future has yet been taken. How much longer can a decision be delayed? For all we know, it may already be too late to meet some plausible contingencies of the medium-term future. Experts differ, but any synthetic fuels industry will need from 10 years to 30 years for investment build-up, after the research and the demonstration development are done. There is certainly no time to lose.

REFERENCES

Antal, M. J. 1982. "Biomass pyrolysis: A review of literature. Part 1—Carbohydrate pyrolysis," *Advances in Solar Energy* 1, pp. 61–111.

Argonne National Laboratory. 1985. "Uniform cost-estimation method for biomass production and conversion technologies." ANL/CNSV/-TM 128.

Arnold, L. E. 1978. "Gross yields of rough wood products from a 25-year-old loblolly and short-leaf pine spacing study." University of Illinois at Urbana-Champaign, Department of Forestry, Forestry Research Report 78–7.

Ayres, R. U. 1978. *Resources, Environment, and Economics: Applications of the Materials/Energy Balance Principle.* New York: Wiley.

Ayres, W. A. 1983. "Gasifiers—past, present and future," *Energy from Biomass,* ANL/CNSV-TM–127, Argonne National Laboratory, pp. 13–16.

Baker, E. G., Mitchell, D. H., Mudge, L. K., and Brown, M. D. 1983. "Methanol synthesis gas from wood gasification," *Energy Progress* 3:4, pp. 226–28.

Baker, E. G., Mudge, L. K., and Brown, M. D. 1987. "Steam gasification of biomass with nickel secondary catalysts," *Industrial Engineering Chemical Research* 26:7, pp. 1335–39.

Beaulieu, Yvan, and Goodyear, Terry. 1985. "Potential for ethanol production from agricultural feedstocks for use in alcohol-gasoline blends." Agriculture Canada. Regional Development Branch, Development Policy Directorate.

Beenackers, A. A. C. M., and van Swaaij, W. P. M. 1983. "Methanol from wood. A state of the art review," *Energy from Biomass,* 2d European Community Conference, edited by A. Strub, P. Chartier, and G. Schleser. London and New York: Applied Science Publishers, pp.782–803.

———. 1984. "Methanol from wood," 1–2. *International Journal of Solar Energy* 2, pp. 349–67, 487–519.

Bentley, W. R. 1984. "Wood as energy: An overview," *Argicultural Issues Overview* No. 3. Washington, D.C.: USDA.

Bills, N. L., and Heimlich, R. E. 1984. "Assessing erosion on U.S. cropland: land management and physical features." Washington, D.C.: USDA, ERS, Agricultural Economic Report No. 513.

Binkley, J. K., Tyner, W. E., and Matthews, M. E. 1983. "Evaluating alternative energy policies: An example comparing transportation investments," *The Energy Journal* 4:2, pp. 91–103.

Biomass Chemicals (periodical). Monthly Update. New York: G. V. Olsen Associates, Agribusiness Intelligence.

"Biomass energy. Review article." 1983. The Biomass Panel of the Energy Research Advisory Board, *Solar Energy* 30:1, pp. 1–31.

Biomass for Energy. 1984. Paris: OECD.

Bowersox, T. W., and Ward, W. W. 1976. "Growth and yield of close-spaced, young hybrid poplars," *Forest Science* 22:4, pp. 449–53.

Braddock, R. L. 1986. "Small methanol plant design for use of low Btu gas," *Energy Progress* 6:2, pp. 76–80.

Braden, J. B., and Uchtmann, D. L. 1985. "Agricultural nonpoint pollution control," *Journal of Soil and Water Conservation* 40, pp. 23–26.

Bruwer, J. J., et al. 1981. "Sunflower seed oil as an extender for diesel fuel in agricultural tractors." Republic of South Africa Department of Agriculture.

Buchanan, R. A., Otey, F. H., and Hamerstrand, E. E. 1980. "Multi-use botanochemical crops, an economic analysis and feasibility study," *Industrial Engineering Chemical Products Research and Development* 19:4, pp. 489–96.

Buhner, H., and Kogl, H. 1981. "Möglichkeiten und Grenzen des Einsatzes von Rapsöl als Motorenkraftstoff in der Bundesrepublik Deutschland," *Landbauforschung Völkenrode* 31:4, pp. 213–26.

Bullard, C. W., Penner, P. S., and Pilati, D. A. 1978. "Net energy analysis," *Resources and Energy* 1, pp. 267–313.

Campbell, G. E., and Clark, S. A. 1986. "The literature of biomass energy production. A bibliography." Final report. University of Illinois at Urbana-Champaign, Department of Forestry.

Campbell, G. E., and Majerus, K. A. 1986a. "An economic assessment of short-rotation forestry and herbaceous crop production for energy feedstocks on marginal lands in the Great Lakes region." University of Illinois at Urbana-Champaign, Department of Forestry.

———. 1986b. "Biomass production for energy feedstocks on marginal land in the Great Lakes region." Executive summary. University of Illinois at Urbana-Champaign, Department of Forestry.

Cannell, M. G. R. 1982. *World Forest Biomass and Primary Production Data*. London and New York: Academic Press.

Cat Folks (periodical). Peoria, Illinois: Caterpillar Company.

Chabbert, N., Braun, P., Gurraud, J. P., Arnoux, M., and Palzy, P. 1983. "Productivity and fermentability of Jerusalem artichoke according to harvest date," *Biomass* 3:3, pp. 209–24.

Chambers, R. S. 1979. "The small fuel-alcohol distillery: General description and economic feasibility workbook." Urbana, Illinois: ACR Process Corporation.

Chambers, R. S., Herendeen, R. A., Joyce, J. J., and Penner, P. S. 1979. "Gasohol: does or or doesn't it produce positive net energy?" *Science* 206, November, pp. 789–95.

Chang, C. D. 1983. *Hydrocarbons from Methanol*. New York and Basel: Marcel Dekker.

Chemical Engineering (periodical).

Chen, N. Y., Degnan, T. F., and Koenig, L. R. 1986. "Liquid fuel from carbohydrates," *Chemtech*, August, pp. 506–11.

Christensen, D. A., Turhollow, A. F., Heady, E. O., and English, B. C. 1983. "Soil loss associated with alcohol production from corn grain and corn residue." CARD Report 115, The Center for Agricultural and Rural Development, Iowa State University, Ames, Iowa.

Cleveland, C. J., Costanza, Robert, Hall, C. A. S., and Kaufman, Robert. 1984. "Energy and the U.S. economy: A biophysical perspective," *Science* 225, August, pp. 890–97.

Cohen, L. H., and Muller, H. L. 1984. "Economics of methanol as a motor fuel." 1984 Fuels and Lubricants Meeting, November 8–9, Houston, Texas (cited from U.S. Congress, 1986a, see below, pp. 153–73).

Collins, R. A., and Headly, J. C. 1983. "Optimal investment to reduce the decay of an investment stream: The case of conservation," *Journal of Environmental Economics and Management* 10, pp. 60–71.

Colwell, H. T. M. 1983. "The potential for a sustained energy supply from combustible crop residues in the Canadian agriculture and food system," *Agriculture Canada*, April.

Commoner, Barry. 1979. *The Politics of Energy*. New York: Knopf.

Cook, E. 1976. "Limits to exploitation of nonrenewable resources," *Science* 191, February, pp. 677–82.

Crow, Patrick. 1987. "Rising U.S. oil imports get attention but not action," *Oil and Gas Journal* July 6, pp. 14–17.

Cushman, J. H., Turhollow, A. F., and Johnston, J. W. 1986. "Herbaceous energy crops: Annual progress report for FY 1986." Oak Ridge National Laboratory, Environmental Sciences Division, Publication No. 2686.

———. 1987. "Herbaceous energy crops program, Annual report for FY 1986." Oak Ridge National Laboratory, Environmental Sciences Division, Publication No. 6369.

David, M. L. 1980. Small-scale fuel alcohol production. Washington, D.C.: USDA.

David, M. L., Hammaker, G. S., Buzenberg, R. J., and Wagner, J. P. 1978. *Gasohol: Economic Feasibility Study*. Washington, D.C.: U.S. Department of Energy, SAN–1681-T1.

Dawson, D. H., Isebrands, J. G., and Gordon, J. C. 1975. "Growth, dry weight yields, and specific gravity of 3-year-old *Populus* growth under intensive culture." USDA, Forest Service, Research Paper NC–122.7.

Dawson, J. O. 1979. "Nitrogen-fixing trees and shrubs," *Illinois Research*, fall, pp. 8–9.

De Zeeuw, J. W. 1978. "Peat and the Dutch Golden Age. The historical meaning of energy-attainability," *A. A. G. Bijdragen* 21, Wageningen, pp. 3–31.

Doering, O. C., and Tyner, W. E. 1980. "Alcohol production from agricultural products: An update on the facts and issues." Lafayette, Indiana: Co-operative Extension Service, Purdue University, EC–511.

Dovring, Folke. 1974. "Inflation feeds on gasoline," *Illinois Business Review* 31:9, October, pp. 6–8.

Dovring, Folke. 1979. "Cropland reserve for fuel production." Report to the Alcohol Fuels Policy Review. Raw material availability report, DOE/ET–0114/1 (National Technical Information Service).

———. 1980. "Export or burn? American grain and the energy equations," *Illinois Business Review* 37:4, May, pp. 9–12.

———. 1981a. "Transportation fuels inflation," *Illinois Business Review* 38:1, February, pp. 8—10, 12.

———. 1981b. "The oil crisis: A case of American underdevelopment," *Illinois Business Review* 38:3, April, pp. 1–3, 7, 11.

———. 1981c. "Energy production and natural resource trade-offs." In *Economics, Ethics, Ecology: Roots of Productive Conservation*, edited by J. W. Jeske. Ankeny, Iowa: Soil Conservation Society of America.

———. 1982a. "Effects of an alcohol fuels program on farm economics." In *Agriculture as a Producer and Consumer of Energy*, edited by W. Lockeretz. AAAS Selected Symposium 78. Boulder, Colorado: Westview Press, for the American Association for the Advancement of Science.

———. 1982b. "Land potential for biomass production in Illinois." University of Illinois at Urbana-Champaign, Department of Agricultural Economics, Staff Paper 82 E–234, mimeo.

———. 1983. "Area measurements in Illinois." *Transactions of the Illinois Academy of Sciences* 75:3/4, pp. 239–46.

———. 1984a. *Energy Use for Midwest Agriculture*. University of Illinois, Department of Agricultural Economics, Agricultural Economics Research Report (AERR) No. 194.

———. 1984b. *Riches to Rags. The Political Economy of Social Waste*. Cambridge, Massachusetts: Schenkman.

———. 1985. "Marginal cost of export crops: The case of corn." University of Illinois at Urbana-Champaign, Department of Agricultural Economics, Staff Paper 85 E–336.

———. 1987a. "Marginal cost of export crops: Wheat, sorghum and rice." University of Illinois at Urbana-Champaign, Department of Agricultural Economics, Staff Paper 87 E–375.

———. 1987b. "Marginal cost of export crops: Soybeans, cotton and tobacco." University of Illinois at Urbana-Champaign, Department of Agricultural Economics, Staff Paper 87 E–378.

———. 1987c. *Productivity and Value. The Political Economy of Measuring Progress*. New York: Praeger.

———. 1987d. "By faith and credit: Economic growth in the 1980s," *Illinois Business Review*, October, pp. 10–13.

———. 1987e. *Land Economics*. Boston, Massachusetts: Breton Publishers (PSW-Kent).

Dovring, Folke, Herendeen, Robert, Plant, Randall, and Ross, M. A. 1980. "Fuel alcohol from grain: Energy and dollar balances of small ethanol distilleries and their economies of size and scale." University of Illinois at Urbana-

Champaign, Department of Agricultural Economics, Staff Paper 80 E–151.

Dovring, Folke, and Yanagida, J.F. 1979. *Monoculture and Productivity.* University of Illinois at Urbana-Champaign, Department of Agricultural Economics, AE 4477.

Dupont, René, and Degand, P. R. 1986. "Make pure H_2 from methanol," *Hydrocarbon Processing*, July, pp. 45–46.

Ecklund, E. E., et al. 1978. "Comparative automotive engine operation when fueled with ethanol and methanol." Washington, D.C.: U.S. Department of Energy, HCP/W1737–01, UC–96.

Edwards, M., and Avidan, A. 1986. "Conversion models aid scale-up of Mobil's fluid-bed MTG process," *Chemical Engineering Science* 41:4, pp. 828–35.

Eigel, R. A., Wittwer, R. F., and Carpenter, S. B. 1978. "Biomass and nutrient content of young black locust stands established by direct seeding on surface mines in eastern Kentucky," *Proceedings*, Third Meeting, Central Hardwoods Forest Conference, pp. 337–46.

Energy Research Abstracts (twice-monthly). Washington, D.C.: U.S. Department of Energy, Office of Scientific and Technical Information.

English, B. C., Alt, K. F., and Heady, E. O. 1982. "A documentation of the Resource Conservation Act's assessment model of agricultural production, land and water use, and soil loss." Ames, Iowa: Center for Agricultural and Rural Development, Iowa State University, CARD Report 107T.

Ericsson, N. R., and Morgan, Peter. 1978. "The economic feasibility of shale oil," *The Bell Journal of Economics* 9:2, pp. 457–87.

Ervin, C. A., and Ervin, D. E. 1982. "Factors affecting the use of soil conservation practices," *Land Economics* Vol. 50, pp. 277–92.

Ezell, A. W., Lowe, W. I., Murphy, W. K., and Wright, J. A. 1983. "Plantation culture for energy production—the importance of within-species selection," *Wood and Fiber Science* 15:1, pp. 69–73.

FAO 1956. *Uses of Agricultural Surpluses to Finance Economic Development in Under-Developed Countries.* Rome. FAO, 1956, 2d printing 1958 (FAO Commodity Policy Studies, No. 6).

Flemming, R. D., and Bechtold, R. L. 1982. "Gaseous transportation fuels," *Automotive Engineering* 90, August, pp. 64–69.

Fowler, G. L., and Randolph, J. C. 1982. "Issues in land-use planning for synthetic fuels from coal and biomass in the midwestern U.S.A.," *Energy* 7:12, pp. 1027–30.

Fri, R. W. 1987. "Changing times for oil imports and energy policy," *Resources* (Washington, D.C.: Resources for the Future), No. 87, spring, pp. 1–3.

Fuel Alcohol. An Energy Alternative for the 1980s. 1981. Washington, D.C.: U.S. National Alcohol Fuels Commission.

Fuel Alcohol on the Farm. 1980. "A primer on production and use." Washington, D.C.: U.S. National Alcohol Fuels Commission.

Fuel from Farms. 1980. "A guide to small scale ethanol production." Golden, CO: Solar Energy Research Institute for U.S. Department of Energy.

Gabele, P. A., Baugh, J. O., Black, Frank, and Snow, Richard. 1985. "Characterization of emissions from vehicles using methanol and methanol-gasoline blended fuels," *JAPCA, Journal of the Air Pollution Control Association* 35, pp. 1168–75.

Garland, Bill. 1979. "Cutting costs for enhanced recovery," *Petroleum Independent* October, pp. 19–22.

Gever, John, Kaufman, Robert, Skole, David, and Vörösmarty, Charles, 1986. *Beyond Oil. The Threat to Food and Fuel in the Coming Decades.* Cambridge, Massachusetts: Ballinger.

Giertz, J. F., and Heins, A. J. 1984. "Real estate: The legacy of a tax advantage," *Illinois Business Review* 41, June, pp. 6–9.

Gilmore, A. R., and Gregory, R. P. 1974. "Twenty years' growth of loblolly and short-leaf pine planted at various spacings in southern Illinois," *Transactions of the Illinois State Academy of Sciences* 67:1, pp. 38–45.

Goodrich, R. S. 1983. "A synfuels era for the United States?" *Energy Conversion and Management* 23:1, pp. 1–9.

Griskey, R. G. 1986. "The future impact of oil shale and tar sands on world oil production," *Energy Progress* 6:3, September, pp. 165–67.

Guymont, Fr. J., and Alpert, J. E. 1978. "Availability of 'agricultural production wastes' for utilization as a feedstock for the production of alochol fuels." Cambridge, MA: Energy Resources, Inc.

Haggin, Joseph. 1982. "Methanol from biomass draws closer to market," *Chemical and Engineering News*, July 12, pp. 24–25.

———. 1986. "Liquid-phase methanol process promises cost saving," *Chemical and Engineering News* August 4, pp. 21–22.

Hall, C. A. S., and Cleveland, C. J. 1981."Petroleum drilling in the United States: Yield per effort and net energy analysis," *Science* 211, February, pp. 576–79.

Hall, J. V. 1985. "Potential air quality benefits of methanol as a vehicle fuel," *Energy* 10:6, pp. 733–36.

Hamilton, J. D. 1983. "Oil and the macroeconomy since World War II," *Journal of Political Economy* 91:2, April, pp. 228–48.

Hannon, Bruce. 1981. "Energy cost of energy," in *Energy, Economics and the Environment*, edited by H. E. Daly and A. F. Humana. AAAS Selected Symposium. Boulder, Colorado: Westview Press, Chapter 3, pp. 81–108.

Hannon, Bruce, and Perez-Blanco, Horacio. 1979. "Ethanol and methanol as industrial feedstocks." ERG Document No. 268, Energy Research Group, University of Illinois at Urbana-Champaign.

Heid, Walter. 1985. "Plugging in to crop residues," *Farmline* (USDA), March, pp. 4–5.

Heimlich, R. E., and Bills, N. L. 1984. "An improved soil erosion classification for conservation policy," *Journal of Soil and Water Conservation* 39:4, pp. 261–66.

Herendeen, R. A., and Brown, Sandra. 1987. "A comparative analysis of net energy from woody biomass," *Energy* 12:1, pp. 75–84.

Herendeen, R. A., and Dovring, Folke. 1984. *Liquid Fuel from Illinois Sources.* University of Illinois at Urbana-Champaign, Department of Agricultural Economics, AERR 192, May.

Herendeen, R. A., and Reidenbach, David. 1982. "Ethanol from grain: Economic balances of small scale production,." University of Illinois at Urbana-

Champaign, Department of Agricultural Economics, Staff Paper 82 E–222.

Herman, M. J. 1981a. *Energy from Biological Material Report.* Washington, D.C.: U.S. Congress, Publications Office, Office of Technology Assessment (OTA).

―――. 1981b. "Food and Fuel: Raw material availability for the United States alcohol fuels program." Washington, D.C.: U.S. Department of Energy.

Hertzmark, Donald, Flaim, Silvio, Ray, Darryll, and Parvin, Greg. 1980. "Economic feasibility of agricultural alcohol production within a biomass system," *American Journal of Agricultural Economics* 62:6, pp. 965–71.

Hoffman, J. J. 1985. "Resinous plants as an economic alternative to bioenergy plantations," *Energy* 10:10, pp. 1139–43.

Houghton-Alico, Doann. 1982. *Alcohol Fuels. Policies, Production, and Potential.* Boulder, Colorado: Westview Press.

Hubbert, M. K. 1974. "World energy resources," in *Tenth Commonwealth Mining and Metallurgical Congress*, Ottawa, Ontario, 1974. Reprinted in *The Wisconsin Seminar on Natural Resource Policies*, Proceedings, 1, Madison, Wisconsin, 1978, pp. 5–93.

Hyman, E. L. 1984. "Land-use planning to help sustain tropical forest resources," *World Development* 12:8, pp. 837–47.

Jantzen, Don, and McKinnon, Tom. 1980. "Preliminary energy balance and economics of a farm-scale ethanol plant." Golden, Colorado: Solar Energy Research Institute for U.S. Department of Energy, SERI/RR–624–669R.

Junge, D. C. 1981. "The state of the arts of producing synthetic fuels from biomass," in *Alternative Energy Sources*, edited by J. T. Manassah. Part A. New York: Academic Press, pp. 251–53, 317–30.

Keene, J. C. 1983. "Managing agricultural pollution," *Ecology Law Quarterly* 11, pp. 135–88.

Keller, J. L., Nakaguchi, G. M., and Ware, J. C. 1978. "Methanol fuel modification for highway vehicle use." Final report. Washington, D.C.: U.S. Department of Energy, HCP/W1683–18.

Kennedy, H. E. 1980. "Coppiced sycamore yields through 9 years." U.S. Department of Agriculture, Forestry Research Service, Research Note S–193–3, Southern Experiment Station, New Orleans.

Keplinger, H. F. 1986. "The crisis in energy is here now!" *World Oil*, June, pp. 52–54, 86.

Kerr, R. A. 1981. "How much oil? It depends on whom you ask," *Science* 212, April, pp. 427–29.

Klass, D. L. 1974. "A perpetual methane economy—Is it possible?" *Chemtech*, March, pp. 161–68.

―――. 1985. "Energy from biomass and wastes: A review and 1983 update," *Resources and Conservation* 11, pp. 157–239.

―――. 1987. "Energy from biomass and wastes: 1985 update and review," *Resources and Conservation* 15, pp. 7–84.

Koch, Peter. 1980. "Concept for southern pine plantation operation in the year 2000," *Journal of Forestry*, February, pp. 78–82.

Kramer, R. A., McSweeny, W. T., and Stavros, R. W. 1983. "Soil conservation with uncertain revenue and input supplies," *American Journal of Agricultural Economics* 65, pp. 694–702.

Krenz, R. O., and Garst, G. D. 1985. "Practices and costs on land placed in crop reduction programs." Stillwater, Oklahoma: Agricultural Economics Department, Oklahoma State University, AE No. 8527.

Krieger, J. H. 1986. "U.S. viewed as unprepared for next energy crisis," *Chemistry and Engineering* June 23, pp. 39–42.

Lipinsky, E. S., Jackson, D. R., Kresovich, S., Arthur, M. F., and Lawhon, W. T. 1979. "Research report on carbohydrate crops as a renewable resource for fuels production." Washington, D.C.: U.S. Department of Energy.

Lovins, A. B. 1976. "Energy strategy: The road not taken," *Foreign Affairs* 55, pp. 65–96.

———. 1977. *Soft Energy Paths: Toward a Durable Peace*. New York: Harper and Row.

Lovins, A. B., and Lovins, L. H. 1982. *Brittle Power: Energy Strategy for National Security*. Andover, Massachusetts: Brick House Publishing.

Lovins, A. B., Lovins, L. H., Krause, Florentin, and Bach, Wilfrid. 1981. *Least-Cost Energy: Solving the CO_2 Problem*. Andover, Massachusetts: Brick House Publishing.

Macnaughton, N. J., Pinto, A., and Rogerson, P. L. 1984. "Development of methanol technology for future fuel and chemical markets," *Energy Progress* 4:4, December pp. 232–41.

Majerus, K. A. 1986a. "Herbaceous energy crop production systems for marginal land in the Great Lakes region." Department of Forestry, University of Illinois at Urbana-Champaign, mimeo.

———. 1986b. "Short-rotation wood production systems for marginal land in the Great Lakes region." Department of Forestry, University of Illinois at Urbana-Champaign, mimeo.

Marsden, S. S., Jr. 1983. "Methanol as a viable energy source in today's world," *Annual Review of Energy*, No. 8, pp. 333–54.

Marten, G. G. 1982. "Land-use issues in biomass energy planning," *Resources Policy* 8:1, March, pp. 65–74.

Mayer, L. V., Heady, E. O., and Holst, D. H. 1965. "Costs of marginal land retirement programs." Ames, Iowa: Center for Agricultural and Economic Development, CARD Report No. 23, mimeo.

McConnell, W. V. 1984. "Options in energy wood farming," *Southern Journal of Applied Forestry* 8:3, pp. 147–52.

McElroy, A. D., Tinberg, Cynthia, Davis, Michael, Snyder, Michael, and Allen, A. D. 1979. "Continuation of systems study of fuels from grasses and grains: Phase 2 and Phase 3." Final report. Golden, Colorado: U.S. Department of Energy, Solar Research Institute.

McGeer, Patrick, and Durbin, Enoch, eds. 1982. *Methane. Fuel for the Future*. New York and London: Plenum Press.

McLaughlin, S. P., and Hoffmann, J J. 1982. "Survey of biocrude-producing plants from the Southwest," *Economic Botany* 36:3, pp. 323–39.

McLaughlin, S. P., Kingsolver, B. E., and Hoffmann, J. J. 1983. "Biocrude production in arid lands," *Economic Botany* 37:2, pp. 150–58.

Meekhoff, Ronald, Gill, Mohinder, and Tyner, Wallace, 1980. *Gasohol. Prospects and Implications.* Washington, D.C.: National Economics Division, ESCS, USDA, Agricultural Economic Report No. 458.

Menard, H. W., and Sharman, George. 1975. "Scientific uses of random drilling models," *Science* 190, No. 4212, October 24, pp. 337–43.

Menrad, H. Decker, G., and Wegener, R. 1983. "The potential of methanol and LPG as new fuels for transportation," *Resources and Conservation* 10, pp. 125–33.

Meridian Corporation. 1986. "Short-rotation intensive culture of woody crops for energy: Principles and practices for the Great Lakes region." Prepared for Great Lakes Regional Biomass Energy Program, Council of Great Lakes Governors, Madison, Wisconsin.

Mineral Facts and Problems. 1980. Washington, D.C.: U.S. Department of the Interior, Bureau of Mines, Bulletin 671.

Mitchell, T. E., Schroer, B. J., Ziemke, M. C., and Peters, J. F. 1983. "Biomass fuels: A national plan," *Chemtech*, April, pp. 242–49.

MITRE. 1979. "Potential availability of wood as a feedstock for methanol production." The MITRE Corporation, Metrek Division, manuscript.

Mudge, L. K., Baker, E. G., Mitchell, D. H., and Brown, M. D. 1985. "Catalytic steam gasification of biomass for methanol and methane production," *Transactions of the ASME—Journal of Solar Energy Engineering* 107, February, pp. 88–92.

Murray, Alan. 1987."Needed: A national energy debate," *Time Magazine,* June 1.

Murray, T. J. 1982. "Issues on government incentives for synthetic fuels from coal and biomass resources in the midwestern U.S.A.," *Energy* 7:12, pp. 1031–32.

National Petroleum News (monthly). Des Plaines, Illinois: Hunter.

A National Plan for Energy Research, Development and Demonstration. 1976. Washington, D.C.: Energy Research and Development Administration, Vol. 1, *The Plan.*

Naylor, L. M., and Schmidt, E. J. 1986. "Agricultural use of wood ash as a fertilizer and liming material," *Tappi Journal*, October, pp. 114–19.

Nehring, Richard, and Van Driest, E. R. 1981. "The discovery of significant oil and gas fields in the United States." Santa Monica, California: The RAND Corporation.

Nelson, D. A., Molton, P. M., Russell, J. A., and Hallen, R. T. 1984. "Application of direct thermal liquefaction for the conversion of cellulosic biomass," *Industrial Engineering Chemical Products Research and Development* 23:3, March, pp. 471–75.

Netschert, Bruce. 1958. *The Future Supply of Oil and Gas.* Baltimore: The Johns Hopkins University Press.

Nicol, K. J., Heady, E. O., and Madsen, H. C. 1974. "Models of soil loss, land and water use, spatial agricultural structure, and the environment." Ames, Iowa: The Center for Agricultural and Rural Development, Iowa State University, CARD Report 49T.

Noon, Randall. 1980. "The potential of butanol," *Gasohol U.S.A.*, December.

Nowak, P. 1983. "Obstacles to the adoption of conservation tillage," *Journal of Soil and Water Conservation* 38, pp. 162–65.

Oil and Gas Journal (weekly). Tulsa, Oklahoma: Penn Well.

Pagoulatos, A., Debertin, D., and Pagoulatos, E. 1978. "Government price policies and availability of crude oil," *The Western Journal of Agricultural Economics*, July, pp. 59–73.

Palmer, E. R. 1984. "Gasification of wood for methanol production," *Energy in Agriculture* 3, pp. 363–75.

Penner, Peter. 1981. "A dynamic input-output analysis of net energy effects in single-fuel economies," *Energy Systems and Policy* 5:2, pp. 89–116.

Perez-Blanco, Horacio, and Hannon, Bruce. 1982. "Net energy analysis of methanol and ethanol production," *Energy* 7:3, pp. 267–80.

Perlack, R. D., Ranney, J. W., Barron, W. F., Cushman, J. H., and Trimble, J. L. 1986. "Short-rotation intensive culture for the production of energy feedstocks in the United States: A review of experimental results and remaining obstacles to commercialization." *Biomass* 9, pp. 145–59.

Perspectives on Prime Lands. 1975. Background papers for seminar on the retention of prime lands, July 16–17, 1975. Washington, D.C.: U.S. Department of Agriculture.

Petroleum Economist (monthly). London: Petroleum Press Bureau.

The Petroleum Situation (monthly). 1977–1981. New York: Chase Manhattan Bank.

Pimentel, David, Fried, C., et al. 1984. "Environmental and social costs of biomass energy," *BioScience* 34:2, February, pp. 89–94.

Pindyck, R. S. 1978. "Gains to producers from cartelization of exhaustible resources," *Review of Economics and Statistics*, 60, May, pp. 238–51.

Pryde, P. R. 1983. *Nonconventional Energy Resources.* New York and Silver Spring, Maryland: Wiley and V. H. Winston.

Ranney, J. W., et al. 1985a. "Short-rotation woody crops program: Annual report for 1984." Oak Ridge, Tennessee: Oak Ridge National Laboratory, ORNL–6160.

———. 1985b. "Specialized hardwood crops for energy and fiber," *Tappi Journal* 68:12, pp. 36–41.

———. 1986a. "Short-rotation woody crops program: Annual progress report for 1985." Oak Ridge, Tennessee: Oak Ridge National Laboratory, Environmental Sciences Division, Publication No. 2541.

———. 1986b. "Research on short-rotation woody crops in the South." In *Biomass Energy Development*, edited by W. H. Smith, pp. 71–84.

Ranney, J. W., Wright, L. L., and Layton, P. A. 1987. "Hardwood energy crops: The technology of intensive culture," *Journal of Forestry*, September, pp. 17–28.

Ranney, J. W., et al. 1987. "Short rotation woody crops program: Annual report for 1986." Oak Ridge, Tennessee: Oak Ridge National Laboratory, for the U.S. Department of Energy.

Rebeiz, C. A., et al. 1983. "Chlorophyll *a* biosynthetic route," *Molecular and Cellular Biochemistry* 57, pp. 97–125.

Rose, D., Ferguson, K., Lothmer, D., and Zavitkowski, J. 1981. "An economic and energy analysis of poplar intensive cultures in the lake states." Research Paper NC 196, North-Central Forest Experiment Station, U.S. Forest Service.

Saterson, K. A., Luppold, M. K., Scow, K. M. and Lee, R. E. 1979. "Herbaceous species screening program. Phase 1." Final report. Washington, D.C.: U.S. Department of Energy. COO–5035–3.

Saucier, J., Clark, A., and McAlpine, R. 1971. "Above-ground biomass yields of short rotation sycamore," *Wood Science* 5, pp. 1–6.

Schnittker Associates. 1980. *Ethanol: Farm and Fuel Issues.* U.S. Alcohol Fuels Commission.

Shen, S. Y., Stavrou, J., Nelson, C. H., and Vyas, A. 1982. "Energy from biomass: Land analysis and evaluation of supply models." Argonne National Laboratory, for U.S. Department of Energy. ANL/CNSV–32, mimeo.

Shen, S. Y., Vyas, A. D., and Jones, P. C. 1984. "Economic analysis of short and ultra short rotation forestry," *Resources and Conservation* 10, pp. 255–70.

Singer, Mark. 1985. *Funny Money.* New York: Knopf.

Smil, Vaclav, 1983. *Biomass Energies. Resources, Links, Constraints.* London and New York: Plenum Press.

Smith, J. L. 1980. "A probabilistic model of oil discovery," *The Review of Economics and Statistics*, pp. 587–94.

Smith, W. H., ed. 1986. *Biomass Energy Development.* New York and London: Plenum Press.

Smith, W. R., ed. 1982. *Energy from Forest Biomass.* New York: Academic Press.

Solar Energy Research Institute. 1980. *Fuels from Farms.* Washington, D.C., SERI/SP–451–519.

Sourie, J. C., and Killen, L. 1986. *Biomass: Recent Economic Studies.* London and New York: Elsevier.

Sperhac, R. G., et al. 1986. "Recommendations for a U.S. synthetic fuels policy," *Energy Progress* 6:4, December, pp. 197–99.

Sperling, Daniel. 1984. "An analytical framework for siting and sizing biomass fuel plants," *Energy* 9:11–12, pp. 1033–40.

———. 1985. "Testing the validity of the soft/hard energy framework: Biomass fuels for transportation," *Transportation Research* 19A:3, pp. 227–42.

Stevens, D. J., and Schiefelbein, G. F. 1985. "Direct conversion of biomass to liquids by thermal processes," *Proceedings of the Summer Meeting of the American Society of Agricultural Engineers*, p. 12 (microfiche).

Strub, A., Chartier, P., and Schleser, G., eds. 1983. *Energy from Biomass.* 2d E. C. Conference. London and New York: Applied Science Publishers.

Sundberg, K., and Mead, S. J. 1983. "Market effectiveness of state government incentives for liquid fuel from biomass," *Energy in Agriculture* 2, pp. 277–83.

Trotter, P. C. 1986. "Biotechnology and the economic productivity of commercial forests," *Tappi Journal*, July, pp. 22–28.

Turhollow, A. F., Christensen, D. A., and Heady, E. O. 1984. "The potential impacts of large-scale fuel alcohol production from corn, grain sorghum, and crop residues under varying technologies and crop export levels." Ames, Iowa: The Center for Agricultural and Rural Development, Iowa State University, CARD Report 126.

Tyner, W. E., Binkley, J. K., Matthews, M. F., and Whitford, R. K. 1981.*Transportation Energy Futures. Paths of Transition.* Vol. 2. Benefits and Costs. Automotive Transportation Center and Department of Agricultural Economics, Purdue University, Lafayette, Indiana, for U.S. Department of Energy.

Update 80 (and other years). Research reports of the Dixon Springs Agricultural Center, University of Illinois (in Pope County, Illinois).

U.S. Congress. 1980. *Energy from Biological Processes.* Vols. 1 and 2; Summary. Office of Technology Assessment, Washington, D.C.

U.S. Congress. 1984. *Methanol Fuel: Kicking the Gasoline Habit.* Proceedings of a seminar sponsored by the Congressional Research Service, November 1984. 98th Congress, 2d Session, Committee Print 09-EE.

U.S. Congress. 1986a. *Methanol—Fuel of the Future.* Hearing before the Subcommittee on Fossil and Synthetic Fuels of the Committee on Energy and Commerce, House of Representatives, 99th Congress, 1st Session, on H.R. 3355, November 1985, Serial No. 99–91.

U.S. Congress. 1986b. *Alcohol Fuels and Lead Phasedown.* A report prepared by the Congressional Research Service. Washington, D.C.: U.S. Government Printing Office, August 1986, 99th Congress, 2d Session, Committee Print 99-HH.

U.S. Department of Agriculture (annual). *Agricultural Outlook.* Washington, D.C.

U.S. Department of Agriculture (periodical). *Agricultural Resources.* Washington, D.C.

U.S. Department of Agriculture (various years). FEDS, Firm Enterprise Data System, estimates of costs and returns to crop livestock production, by production areas.

U.S. Department of Agriculture. 1959. *A Fifty-Year Look Ahead at U.S. Agriculture.* Washington, D.C.

U.S. Department of Agriculture. 1980. *Small Scale Alcohol Fuel Production.* Washington, D.C.: U.S. Government Printing Office.

U.S. Department of Agriculture. 1981a. The *National Agricultural Lands Study.* Washington, D.C.: U.S. Department of Agriculture.

U.S. Department of Agriculture. 1981b. *1980 Appraisal. Soil, Water, and Related Resources in the United States.* 2 parts. Washington, D.C.

U.S. Department of Agriculture. 1983. *A Biomass Energy Production and Use Plan for the United States, 1983–1990.* Washington, D.C.: Agricultural Economic Report No. 505. (Joint with U.S. Department of Energy.)

U.S. Department of Agriculture. 1986. *1985 Agricultural Chart Book*, USDA Agricultural Handbook No. 652. Washington, D.C.

U.S. Department of Energy. 1979. *The Report of the Alcohol Fuels Policy Review.* Washington, D.C.: DOE/PE–0012.

Vyas, A. D., and Shen, S. Y. 1982. "Analysis of short-rotation forests using the Argonne model for selecting economic strategy (MOSES)." Argonne, Illinois: Argonne National Laboratory.

Wan, Edward. 1978. "A plan for the introduction of biomass-based methanol into the energy economy." In *Proceedings of the Second Annual Symposium on Fuels from Biomass*, June 2–22 (at) Rensselaer Polytechnic Institute, Troy, New York. U.S. Department of Energy, CONF–7806107-P1, pp. 126–50.

Webb, S. E. H., Ogg, C. W., and Huang, W. Y. 1986. "Idling erodible cropland:

Impacts on production, prices, and government costs." USDA Agricultural Economic Report 550. Washington, D.C.: USDA.

Weisz, P. B., and Marshall, J. F. 1979. "High-grade fuels from biomass farming: Potentials and constraints," *Science*, October 5, pp. 57–8.

Wentworth, T. O., and Othmer, D. F. 1982. "Producing methanol for fuels," *Chemical Engineering Progress*, August, pp. 29–36.

White, E. H., and Hook, D. D. 1975. "Establishment and regeneration of silage plantings," *Iowa State Journal of Research*, 49, pp. 287–96.

"Wood Residue as an Energy Source." 1976. Madison, Wisconsin: Forest Products Research Society, Proceedings, No. P–75–13.

Wood, B. W., Carpenter, S. B., and Wittwer, R. F. 1976. "Intensive culture of American sycamore in the Ohio River Valley," *Forest Science* 22:3, pp. 338–42.

Yoon, H., Stouffer, M. R., Dudt, P. J., Burke, F. P., and Curran G. P. 1985. "Methanol dissociation for fuel use," *Energy Progress* 5:2, June, pp. 78–83.

Young, J., Griffin, E., and Russell, J. 1986. "Feasibility of biomass-based fuels and chemical production in the USA," *Biomass* 10, pp. 9–25.

Zeimetz, K. A. 1979. *Growing Energy, Land for Biomass Farms*. Washington, D.C.: USDA, ESCS, Agricultural Economic Report No. 125.

INDEX

acid rain, 129
acreage reserve program, 61
aldehydes, 114, 116
alder, 86
alfalfa, 44, 77, 84, 89, 95
allothermal techniques, 99
American Automobile Association, 132
American Gas Association, 114
Amoco, 114
analog foods, 64
anthracite, 6, 20
Argonne National Laboratory, 85, 90, 92
artificial chlorophyll, 4, 16, 17–18, 31
ashes, 76–79, 86, 89–90
Atlantic Richfield (ARCO), 122, 130
autothermal techniques, 99, 104
aviation fuel, 125, 127

bagasse, 35
Bank of America, 121
Bermuda grass, 84
biocrude crops, 85
black locust, 86
bluestem, 84
breeder reactors, 26–27

Brookhaven National Laboratory, 100
butyl alcohol, 30, 37, 39

California Energy Commission, 121–22
Caterpillar Company, 118, 131
charcoal making, 99, 114
Chernobyl, 26, 129
coal liquefaction, 20–21, 128
coking gas, 20
cold start, 14, 114, 117–18, 120
Conoco, 115, 130
Conservation Reserve Program, 48–49, 71–72, 82, Table 5.2
contour plowing, 70
corn sweeteners, 63
corrosiveness, 114, 117, 119
cottonwood, 86
crop residues, 34, 75

decontrol of petroleum prices, 10, 13
Department of Energy, 16, 29, 121, 128–29
deuterium, 16, 24, 27
dietary habits, 47

dissociation burning, 99, 103, 115, 118, 126–27
distillers' dry grain (DDG), 39, 42–43, 57, 74
doomsayers, 7
Douglas fir, 88
dust bowl, 68

energy costs (of fuel), 38, 56–58, 103–5
enhanced recovery, 10–11
Environmental Protection Agency, 116
etna, 33, 118
eucalyptus, 86
export crops, 53
Exxon Company, 107
Ezekiel, Mordecai, 59

FEDS. *See* Firm Enterprise Data System
fescue, 84
Firm Enterprise Data System (FEDS), 54, 76, 89, 92–93
Fischer-Tropsch technique, 102, 104
fission fragments, 25
flash pyrolysis, 102
flexible fuel vehicle (FFV), 119
food aid, 58–59
Ford Escort, 119, 121
Ford Motor Company, 119–20, 131
fusel oils, 39
fusion energy, 27

gama grass, 84
gasohol, 22, 29, 33–35, 41, 74, 106, 118–19, 129, 132
Gramm-Rudman Act, 129
grassy waterways, 34, 70
greasing of factory machines, 7
green revolution, 60
greenhouse effect, 4, 18, 21–22
groundwater mining, Figure 6.2
gulley erosion, 68–69

heat islands, 18
hemicellulose, 98

Hubbert, M. King, 9–11, 20
hydropyrolysis, 99

imitation meats, 63
Indianapolis 500, 1, 113
infant industry, 93–96, 125–26
infield drilling, 10, 13
intensive silviculture, 78–79, 81, 85–86, 93, 100
International Harvester, 110
intertemporal choice, 70

Jerusalem artichoke, 44, 77
Johnson grass, 84
joint products, 37, 42–43

kerosene, 7

lead in gasoline, 41
lignin, 36, 98
lime, 77, 89–90
liquefied petroleum gas (LPG), 114
loblolly pine, 87–88
Lovins, A. B., 17

Madison, James, 128
margarine, 47, 63–64
mass transit, 15, 129–30
meat analogs, 64
meat consumption, 63
micro nutrients, 77, 89
MITRE Corporation, 107
Mobil Corporation, 100–102, 104, 130
Mukluk oil field, 11

New Deal, 2
nonpoint pollution, 72

Oak Ridge National Laboratory, 84, 86, 90–91
octane, 37–38, 41
OPEC, 1, 12–14
orchard grass, 84
overthrust zone, 10

Paley Report, 20, 128
panic grass, 84

payment-in-kind (PIK), 48
peat, 6
phase separation, 118–19
pillar forest, 79
pines, 86–87
Pittsburgh Energy Technology Center, 102, 104
plutonium, 24–27
poplars, 85–86, 90, 92
propanol, 37
Prudhoe Bay, 11
Public Law 480, 61
pyrolysis, 89, 99

reed canary grass, 84
rill erosion, 68–69
rural household fuel, 6

scale economies, returns to scale, 109, 111
set-aside land, 3, 49, 62, 71, 82, 95
shale oil, 23
sheet erosion, 68–69
Shippingport, Pennsylvania, 27
short-rotation forestry, 85
sieve materials, 37
size, economies of and returns to, 109, 111
slurry pipelines, 21
Smith, Adam, 128
soft path, 17
Soil Bank, 61–63, 71

solar electricity, 28
South African Synthetic Oil (SASOL), 20–21
South Coast Air Quality Management District, 116
stagflation, 1, 12–13
strip mining, 19
stripper wells, 10, 13
sugar beets, 35
sugar cane, 34–35
summer fallow, 48, 94, Table 5.1
sweet sorghum, 34–35
switchgrass, 84
sycamores, 85, 90, 92

tar sands, 23–24
tertiary oil, 10, 36
thorium, 24, 27
Three Mile Island, 26, 129
toxicity, 98, 114–17

uranium, 16, 24–27

vegetable oils, 30
virgin lands in the Soviet Union, 68

water pollution, 72–74
wind erosion, 68
wind power, 6, 17
windjammers, 6
wood fuel, 28, Table 2.1
wood grass, 85–86, 90–91

ABOUT THE AUTHOR

FOLKE DOVRING was born in Sweden and is a naturalized U.S. citizen. Son of a famous Swedish poet and novelist, he grew up in a rural area. He was tutored by his parents and attended no school before entering Lund University where he studied humanities and social sciences. After earning his Ph.D. he taught economic history at Lund then worked for the United Nations' Food and Agriculture Organization (FAO) as a statistician and economist for several years, mainly at the FAO headquarters in Rome. Since 1960 he has been a professor at the University of Illinois College of Agriculture, teaching land economics and economic development. He has served as a consultant to several international organizations as well as to several government departments in Washington.

Energy problems have been at the center of his work since 1973. His research and writings cover many other areas, from land tenure in medieval Europe to land reform in modern times, productivity, economic growth and development, economic distributions, land values and taxation, and the philosophy of science. His published works have appeared in a dozen languages in as many countries, among them India, Mexico, and the Soviet Union. They include 12 books, including *Land and Labor in Europe* (1956, 3rd rev. ed. 1965); *History as a Social Science* (1960, new ed. as a "historiography classic" 1984); *The Optional Society* (1972); *Riches to Rags* (1984); *Land Economics* (1987); *Productivity and Value* (1987); *Progress for Food—Or Food for Progress* (1988), and a text edition (1952) of Hugo Grotius's classic work on civil law, from a manuscript discovered by Dovring.

The author has traveled widely in the United States, Asia, and Europe.

He speaks several languages fluently and reads most of those spoken in Europe, including Russian. He is listed in *World Who's Who in Science* (Marquis who's who), *American Men and Women of Science*, and *Vem Är Det?* (Swedish who's who).